STANDARD LOAN

2 7 APR 2011

D1346575

2.2009

THE ETHICAL
EXECUTIVE

THE ETHICAL
EXECUTIVE

Avoiding the traps of the
unethical workplace

ROBERT HOYK
PAUL HERSEY

STANFORD
BUSINESS
BOOKS

KOGAN
PAGE

This edition not for sale in the USA (and dependent territories), Canada, South and
Central America.

UNIVERSITY OF CHICHESTER

Publisher's note

First published in the United States in 2008 by Stanford Business Books, an imprint
of Stanford University Press.

First published in Great Britain in 2009 as a co-publication of Stanford Business
Books, an imprint of Stanford University Press, and Kogan Page Limited:

Kogan Page Limited	Stanford University Press
120 Pentonville Road	1450 Page Mill Road
London N1 9JN	Palo Alto, CA 94304
United Kingdom	USA
www.koganpage.com	

British Library Cataloguing in Publication Data

A CIP record for this book is available from the British Library.

ISBN 978 0 7494 5335 0

Designed by Bruce Lundquist
Typeset by Stanford University Press in 10.5/15 Sabon
Printed and bound in India by Replika Press Pvt Ltd

174·
4
HOY

To Julie Brickman,
for her belief in this work and her many hours of editorial magic.
Author Robert Hoyk is honored to be married to Julie and loves
her deeply.

"That line between good and evil is permeable. . . .
Any of us can move across it. . . . I argue that we all have
the capacity for love and evil—to be Mother Theresa,
to be Hitler. . . . It's the situation that brings that out."

PHILIP ZIMBARDO
STANFORD UNIVERSITY

CONTENTS

Trap 30: "We Won't Get Caught" 72

Trap 31: "We Didn't Hurt Them That Bad" 72

Trap 32: Self-Serving Bias 73

Trap 33: Addiction 75

Trap 34: Coworker Reactions 77

Trap 35: Established Impressions 79

Trap 36: Contempt for the Victim 82

Trap 37: Doing Is Believing 85

PART III   PERSONALITY TRAPS

Trap 38: Psychopathy 89

Traps 39 and 40: Poverty and Neglect 92

Trap 41: Low Self-Esteem 94

Trap 42: Authoritarianism 95

Trap 43: Social Dominance Orientation 96

Trap 44: Need for Closure 98

Trap 45: Empathy 100

PART IV   ANALYZING DILEMMAS

The Parable of the Sadhu 105

   Analysis 106

      Lost in the Group 106

      Tyranny of Goals 106

      Time Pressure 107

      Conflicts of Loyalty 107

      Self-Serving Bias 108

      Annihilation of Guilt 108

ACKNOWLEDGMENTS

OUR THANKS to Ron Campbell for linking us together and for his conscientious support. Our appreciation to Jere Calmes and Sharon Daloz Parks for their assistance with the initial proposal. Special thanks to Geoffrey Burn and his dynamic team at Stanford University Press: their enthusiasm, attention to detail, and collaborative genius. We are grateful for the help of Michele Potter and Denice Douglas with permissions. We would also like to acknowledge our astute agent, Rita Rosenkranz.

Robert Hoyk would like to acknowledge Eli Fernandez; Anthony Parinello; Robert Daigneault; and his mother, Rosalyn Heuck, for their encouragement, which set him on the path of writing.

FOREWORD

YOU ARE ONE OF THE LUCKY ONES—you picked up this book! The favor you can do for yourself is to run to the checkout stand (or click and point on-screen), invest your hard-earned money, and buy it. Here's why:

On each and every page you'll find out why we all from time to time have acted in unethical ways. Perhaps knowingly, perhaps not. At the end of the day, it all boils down to how acting unethically ultimately effects or infects our self-esteem and self-worth.

ON THE WAY TO SCHOOL, Erin's cell phone rang (go figure). Her best friend had just broken up with her boyfriend, and she asked Erin to skip the first class of the day to comfort her. Reluctantly, Erin agreed, and they met at the local coffee house. Erin, a 4.0 GPA student and senior class president, was promptly busted, which led to a three-day suspension and a request from the school principal to step down from the position of class president because of her unethical behavior. On top of that, her parents pulled her cell phone for four weeks and grounded her for the same period of time (four weeks is like a lifetime to a teenager).

AN ETHICAL TRAP OF SORTS
What happened to Erin on her way to school happens to each and every one of us each and every day—we find ourselves in a trap of

sorts. What really matters is how we respond to traps, a response that will make either deposits or withdrawals in our self-esteem bank account and either honor ethics or put them at risk. And as with a well-run, fiscally responsible business, operating in the black versus in the red make the difference in future wealth, stability, growth, reputation, success, and happiness.

Erin's response to her girlfriend's request created a withdrawal—a consequence. Erin's response to that consequence has the power to create either yet another withdrawal or a deposit. Yep, another "trap" has presented itself!

Let's say Erin responds with, "How unfair! What a bust! What an over-reaction! Suspension! Forfeit my presidency . . . after all my hard-work campaigning? And what gives with my parents? Four weeks without a phone! My friends will forget I exist!" And as Erin begins to rebel and fails to see her part in what *she* created, she has just encountered another ethical trap (there are forty-five, to be exact, which you'll be learning all about in the chapters that follow).

This book will not teach you how to be ethical. Instead, and more important, it will educate you to recognize the day-to-day ethical traps that we all face, analyze them, and give the practical, usable information you need to respond in a way that supports good intention, fair decisions, and abundant wealth. Whether you're a CEO, a layperson, an executive, or a manager, knowledge of the traps described in this book will give you chance after chance to make substantial deposits in your self-esteem bank account.

Oh, one more thought: after you read this book, give it to the people you love the most and have them read it. You'll be glad you did.

Anthony Parinello,
author of Think & Sell Like a CEO

THE ETHICAL EXECUTIVE

TRAPPED!

IN THE WINTER OF 2001, Enron, the seventh largest company in the Fortune 500, went bankrupt. It was the second largest bankruptcy in the history of the United States. The Justice Department began an investigation after Enron admitted to fraudulent accounting that had overstated its income by $586 million. With the meltdown of the company, the loss to investors exceeded $60 billion.[1]

In the spring of 2002, Adelphia Communications, one of the largest cable companies in America, filed bankruptcy after restating its profits. The founder of the company, John Rigas, and his three sons had already been indicted. It was alleged that the Rigas family had used assets of their company as collateral to acquire personal loans of $3.1 billion.[2] Recently, John Rigas was sentenced to fifteen years in prison, and his son Timothy Rigas was sentenced to twenty years in prison. They were convicted on charges of looting company funds to the tune of $2.3 billion.[3]

In the summer of 2002, the CEO of Tyco International, Dennis Kozlowski, was indicted for evading sales tax totaling $1 million. After continued investigations by the district attorney, Kozlowski and two other executives were accused of siphoning off $600 million of company money into their own pockets.[4]

Both Kozlowski and Mark Swartz, CFO of Tyco, received prison sentences of eight to twenty-five years for looting $150 million in company funds.[5]

Without a doubt, the executives involved in these scandals had to be evil! They must have been psychopaths, leaders who would stop at nothing, leaders with criminal minds.

Perhaps in a few instances leaders who were responsible for scandals such as these were psychopaths. Robert Hare, who developed the Psychopathy Checklist, an instrument used by psychologists to diagnose psychopaths, estimates that 1 percent of people in business could be classified as being psychopathic.[6]

Yet the truth can often be disconcerting. Far more likely, these leaders are no different than you or us. "Impossible!" you say. "I could never scam shareholders out of $60 billion!"

It's much more tidy and reassuring to blame one or two "evil" people. Myths of good and evil permeate our culture—there are the good guys and the bad guys.

One concept that Sigmund Freud pioneered and got right is that our behavior is multi-determined. There are multiple causes for our actions. The way we act is the result of a complex weave of situational factors, history, and personality. With the advent of social psychology, which is the behavior of individuals in groups, we have learned that the influence of the situation often overpowers the influence of personality. Even if we have good ethical values to begin with, given certain situational pressures, every one of us can become unethical.

From the ages of ten to eighteen the primary author of this book, Robert Hoyk, had one passion—magic. He performed for birthday parties, community functions, schools, colleges—he even performed one time at the Magic Castle, a private club for magicians in Hollywood.

Imagine that you're watching one of his favorite close-up tricks. Hoyk borrows a quarter from you. He picks up an empty drinking glass and drops the quarter into the glass. It clatters to the bottom. You're standing only a few feet away from him. He makes several magic passes with his hand and, suddenly, the quarter in the glass moves! It begins to levitate! The quarter slowly crawls up the inside of the glass almost to the rim. Abruptly, the coin drops to the bottom of the glass with a clink. Hoyk gives the coin back to you and you turn it over looking for any signs of tampering. None are evident.

How was the trick done? Hoyk used a long, fine, human hair. At each end was a small pellet of wax. One end was attached to his belt with the wax; the other end was lightly stuck to his thumb. When he borrowed the coin he stuck the pellet of wax to one side of the coin—the side opposite your view. With the coin at the bottom of the glass, all he needed to do was very slowly move the glass away from his body and the coin rose in the glass. Really, the coin didn't move—it was the glass that moved. But the coin looked like it was floating up the inside of the glass.

When you know how the trick is done, you clearly see the fine hair attached to the coin. You see the hair running up the inside of the glass, over the rim, and horizontally to Hoyk's belt. *Once you're aware of the hair, it's hard to believe that you didn't see it before. You can see it plain as day once you know it's there.* With awareness, illusions are just magic tricks that seem obvious. Without awareness, life's illusions trap us and distort our perception.

In this book, we will describe forty-five traps that every one of us falls prey to. Some of these traps distort our perception of right and wrong—so we *actually believe* our unethical behavior is right. The traps are psychological in nature, and if we're not aware of them they are like illusions—webs of deception. Once we see them, like the human hair in the magic trick, they lose much of their power to deceive us and we can more easily navigate around them.

In all likelihood, the traps we'll describe in this book helped to deceive ordinary people and sway them to torture and murder millions of human beings in Hitler's Germany. They probably influenced ordinary people to commit mass suicide and murder their children in Jonestown. In our analysis, these traps significantly contributed to the disasters of Enron, Adelphia, and Tyco.

Let's look at a company that had a tradition of high moral conduct that became trapped. In 2001 and again in 2002, Johnson & Johnson was ranked as the number one company Americans respected and admired. The company's credo states that its foremost responsibility is to the people who use its products. It's obligatory for all employees of this international company to be familiar with its credo.[7]

The credo was developed after the well-known Tylenol case in 1982. Johnson & Johnson recalled from stores thirty-one million containers of Tylenol following the death of eight people. Tylenol capsules had been opened and the ingredients mixed with cyanide. The company was not to blame for the deadly altering of the ingredients. Nonetheless, Johnson & Johnson redesigned the packaging so that in the future the Tylenol capsules could not be tampered with. The recall cost the company close to $2.5 billion in revenues.[8] This case has often been used in textbooks as a prime example of ethical conduct.

Sixteen years after the Tylenol case, LifeScan, a division of Johnson & Johnson, was raided by federal agents. LifeScan manufactured SureStep, a device that diagnosed diabetes. The company had withheld information from the F.D.A. concerning a defect in the software for SureStep. Johnson & Johnson was indicted for criminal charges and pleaded guilty. The company paid $60 million in fines. Ralph Larsen, CEO of the company, stated that the executives at LifeScan "cared deeply about the company's credo."[9] Were these executives evil? More than likely, they were normal people. Probably, they got caught in a trap called *minimizing*, which we'll describe later.

The vast majority of people care about ethics, but are vulnerable to the traps described in this book. Good intentions are not enough to combat these forty-five traps. One of the most important ways to guard against corruption is to understand and be aware of these traps that distort our perceptions.

Knowledge of these forty-five traps will help the individual stay away from corruption. *Voyagers who know the location of quicksand navigate around it.* When we clearly identify danger, we can prepare for it and avoid it. Knowledge of these forty-five traps can give people the awareness that will enable them to make a difference; it will help individuals recognize and stop corruption at its roots—corruption within themselves and their organizations. Moreover, knowledge of these traps will aid individuals at all levels of an organization—from volunteers in nonprofit organizations to CEOs of large companies.

Corruption is widespread. A 2000 survey conducted by an accounting firm established that 49 percent of employees thought that if the misconduct within their business was made known, their organization would "significantly lose public trust."[10] We all work for or belong to organizations. The traps described in this book can erupt in any organization environment.

Three years ago Bernard Ebbers, the CEO of WorldCom, was convicted in a federal court of an $11 billion dollar accounting fraud. He was given a prison sentence of twenty-five years! WorldCom was the largest bankruptcy in the history of the United States.[11] Given the fact that our society is based on organizational systems and that trillions of dollars flow through Wall Street, there will always be a need for awareness of the traps described in this book.

WHY DO TRAPS EXIST, AND WHAT ARE THEY?

TRAPS EXIST because at any given moment in time we have impulses that motivate us to act. These impulses are reactions to internal or external stimuli. Sometimes a stimulus is so powerful or triggers such automatic behavior that we act on it without being aware that other options exist. At other times, we are aware of other choices but the stimulus's effect overrides these potential actions.

Social-psychological traps are similar to fish traps. Fish traps are wire cages that have an entrance shaped like a large funnel that narrows toward the inside of the cage; the special funnel design directs the fish to swim into the trap. In the same way, an individual or organization begins to move in a certain direction. Later, the action turns out to be disastrous without any simple means to reverse course.[1] The essential question to ask is, *What* makes the individual or organization begin to move in the ill-fated direction? The forty-five "traps" in our book are descriptions of the different internal or external stimuli that compel people to begin this movement toward disaster.

For example, the first trap delineated in this book is *obedience to authority*. As children we were all primed to obey our parents. Our survival depended on it. In school this conditioning continued. We automatically knew that we had to show deference to our teachers. Consequently, later in life, as adults, when our boss orders us to do something we quickly obey without thinking.

If a person of authority orders us to do something that is unethical, *obedience to authority* is such a powerful external stimulus that we are prone to obey the order without being aware that we're going against our ethical principles. At other times we might be aware that we're acting unethically but the impulse to obey is so strong it overrides our ethical judgment.

In this book we propose three main categories of traps: Primary, Defensive, and Personality.

Obedience to authority is a Primary Trap. Primary Traps are predominately external stimuli. These are the main traps that have the potential to impel us to move in a certain direction without regard for our ethical principles.

Defensive Traps are in a very different category. Although some of them can at times be included with Primary Traps, these traps are basically attempts to find easy ways to reverse course after a transgression has already been committed. For the most part, Defensive Traps are maneuvers that are reactions to two internal stimuli: guilt and shame. Guilt and especially shame are very painful emotions. They call into question the positive view we have of ourselves. Defensive Traps are insidious because they are often very successful at annihilating or at least minimizing our guilt and shame. They help us deny our transgressions, thus setting us up for repeated unethical behavior.

Personality Traps are exclusively internal stimuli. These traps are various personality traits that can make us more vulnerable to wrongdoing.

It should be noted that at times our behavior is affected by more than one trap simultaneously. Several external traps can influence us at the same time, as can a combination of internal and external traps.

Depending on the context, most traps are benign and can have a positive influence on our lives. For example, *empathy* is often the cornerstone of good ethics. But in some circumstances, this personality trait can actually overpower our sense of fairness. Traps can incite tunnel vision. The pull to act on them is so strong that we can become blinded to other behavioral options. They can lead us and the people we respect and admire, even whole companies, rapidly down the path of corruption.

WHY THIS ISN'T JUST ANOTHER BUSINESS ETHICS BOOK

MANY BOOKS ON BUSINESS ETHICS for the general public teach values or rules; for example, "follow the Golden Rule." But even if we have good ethical values to begin with, we can all become unethical—trapped by the situational pressures and self-deceptions illustrated in this book.

Traditionally, books on ethics used in business schools or for undergraduate courses present vignettes of ethical dilemmas professionals are likely to face in their particular fields, such as pollution, sexual harassment, product safety, and discrimination, which have no clear right or wrong answers. To solve these "grey dilemmas," such books usually outline a process that involves eight to twelve steps based on principles from philosophy. One of the top-selling business ethics texts includes the following process:

Twelve Questions for Examining the
Ethics of a Business Decision
1. Have you defined the problem adequately?
2. How would you define the problem if you stood on the other side of the fence?
3. How did this situation occur in the first place?
4. To whom and to what do you give your loyalty as a person and a member of the corporation?
5. What is your intention in making this decision?

6. How does this intention compare with the probable results?
7. Whom could your decision or action injure?
8. Can you discuss the problem with the affected parties before you make your decision?
9. Are you confident that your position will be as valid over a long period of time as it seems now?
10. Could you disclose without qualm your decision or action to your boss, your CEO, the board of directors, your family, society as a whole?
11. What is the symbolic potential of your action if understood? If misunderstood?
12. Under what conditions would you allow exceptions to your stand?[1]

After reading a vignette that describes an ethical dilemma, the student uses these questions to sort out what's right and wrong—to make the best possible ethical decision.

But can ethics be taught by dilemmas and processes based on philosophical principles? Do traditional courses and textbooks actually make a difference? It's clear that students who have received ethics education, when evaluated by paper-and-pencil instruments such as *The Defining Issues Test*, demonstrate increased moral judgment.[2] What's not clear is whether ethics education actually affects behavior in the work environment.

A little over twelve years ago, Joseph Badaracco, an ethics professor at Harvard Business School, conducted thirty extensive interviews with recent M.B.A. graduates who had faced ethical dilemmas in the business world. All of the thirty managers had taken a class on business ethics at Harvard. About half of them worked for companies that had official ethics programs. Badaracco writes, "[C]orporate ethics programs, codes of conduct, mission statements, hot lines, and the like provided little help . . . the young managers resolved the dilemmas they faced largely on the basis of personal reflection and individual values, not through reliance on corporate credos, company loyalty, the exhortations of senior executives, philosophical principles, or religious reflection." The majority of the Harvard managers had learned their personal values primarily from their family upbringing, not from ethics courses.[3] This study suggests that traditional ethics education that is based on philosophical principles does not transfer to the workplace.

After Badaracco's study, we are not aware of any other research that has attempted to link ethics education with actual behavior in the working world. However, in the past twelve years ethics texts have improved. More and more emphasis is being placed on management ethics, setting up and maintaining an organizational culture that fosters good ethics. *But what is mostly lacking in books on ethics is a major emphasis on the root causes of unethical behavior—psychological dynamics.* In business, people act unethically not because of the conflict between maximizing profits and adhering to laws but because of social-psychological traps. (An emotional investment related to maximizing profits can be one type of trap.)

The history of ethics is based on the utilization of philosophical principles. The precursor of psychology is also philosophy. Psychology was born when philosophical ideas were tempered by empirical science. It's time to acknowledge that philosophy is the forerunner of ethics and to move ethics into the realm of science and social psychology.

Many of the Harvard managers interviewed in Badaracco's study confronted the trap *obedience to authority*; they were overtly told to act unethically by their bosses. For example, one Harvard manager was instructed "to make up data to support a new product introduction. When he began to object, his boss cut him off and said 'Just do it.'" Ordered to act unethically, these entry-level managers experienced intense anxiety. If they didn't obey, they worried that they would lose their boss's support, which was crucial to be "a candidate for the fast track and a team player." Ultimately they worried about destroying their careers and losing their jobs.[4]

Let's look back at the "Twelve Questions for Examining the Ethics of a Business Decision." Are any of these questions relevant to the issues these Harvard managers faced? If the managers had used them, would they have helped? Overall, the "Twelve Questions" would have offered little assistance. Only question 10, "Could you disclose without qualm your decision or action to your boss, your CEO, the board of directors, your family, society as a whole?" is relevant to the resolution style used by the Harvard managers. From the content of the interviews, it's evident that how others perceived their integrity was important to them.[5]

The crucial problem these Harvard managers faced was the intense anxiety that resulted from the trap *obedience to authority*. Emotions can bring us all to our knees. Many of the traps in this book incite powerful emotions that in turn pull us toward wrongdoing.

The "Twelve Questions" would have had no influence over lessening the Harvard managers' intense anxiety, which ultimately would have driven them to act unethically. The managers were able to cope with their anxiety by reassuring themselves that they were still young and their careers were just beginning. They told themselves they could always find work in another company if being ethical resulted in the loss of their jobs. For the most part, the Harvard managers were able to resolve their dilemmas because of this flexibility. They also acknowledged that had they been older, with families and invested status in the company, finding new employment would have been less of an option.[6] So what about middle managers, for instance, who don't have this flexibility, who have spent years climbing the corporate ladder and have a family to support, what do they do when intense anxiety hits?

The anxiety provoked by the trap *obedience to authority* revolves around two issues: career advancement and being considered a team player. It's important to realize that these issues are two additional traps: *conformity* and *self-interest*. (The trap *self-interest* has three subtypes: *tyranny of goals*, *money*, and *conflicts of interest*.) A trap, then, can stir up one or more other traps.

In spite of this, if middle managers have a firm knowledge of the traps in this book, they can use their understanding to objectify what's happening to them. A manager can think about or preferably talk to a friend regarding the nature of the traps he or she is confronted with, their allure, and the possible distortions they evoke. Through this process, a bit of distance is created between the person and his or her worries; and thus the anxiety is lessened. Moreover, the awareness that they're struggling against several traps simultaneously will likely compel managers to slow down and be more cautious, alert, and vigilant. Consequently, their deliberations will be clearer. If middle managers can take the extra time gained from being more cautious and talk about their anxieties sufficiently, a process called desensitization happens and their anxiety is significantly reduced. In general, by retelling something over and over people can emotionally habituate to any type of distress. At this point, the manager is well on the way to avoiding the traps. If the manager's anxiety still remains too high, it is best dealt with by techniques of psychology—skills a psychologist can teach.

Psychology can both explain the nature of traps and structure the approach to avoiding or remediating them. Our book places a major focus on the root causes of unethical behavior—psychological dynamics. It inaugurates a new priority in the field that we hope will lead to a clearer vista and fresh solutions.

A WORD ABOUT RESEARCH

WE USE EXAMPLES of experimental research in this book to support the evidence for the forty-five traps. People often criticize research as not being "the real world." Why don't we just use real-life examples from the business world without research? In the "real world," there are so many influences that happen simultaneously to cause unethical behavior that conclusions are pure guesswork. It is only through research, by strictly controlling the circumstances, that we can take each influence one at a time, without the others, to see if it indeed has an impact.

Moreover, by using research, we can sort out the influence of the situational elements versus the influence of character traits. The influence of the situation often has more power than personalities. Experimental research is a system that sets up tightly controlled circumstances and then looks at the effects of each aspect of a situation on randomly selected people called subjects. When this process is carefully done, we can generalize the results of the experiment to anyone.

When Philip Zimbardo conducted his acclaimed prison study at Stanford University (see Trap 17), he was trying to understand brutality that often erupted in prisons. He speculated that the environment and the "institutional roles" of the prison guards might be a stronger influence on their behavior than who they were as people. *To prove his idea, Zimbardo knew that he had to set up an experiment that used subjects who had never seen the inside of a prison.* He also knew that he had to randomly assign subjects to play the roles of guards and prisoners. Using this methodology, any brutality that erupted in the experiment could be attributed to the environment and the roles enacted.

In the same way, our book is trying to scientifically demonstrate that anyone subjected to particular roles or situations can become trapped and behave unethically. Therefore we have chosen to spotlight true, experimental designs that utilize subjects, as much as possible, from the general population.

More than one friend upon seeing the title of our book, *The Ethical Executive*, has exclaimed, "That's an oxymoron!" By describing experiments in our book that employ non-businesspeople as subjects, we hope to counter this bias and leave the reader with the message that unethical traps are universal and we all fall prey to their influence.

PART I:
PRIMARY TRAPS

This section will describe and explore twenty traps that cause people to behave unethically. These are the main traps that pull us in; the traps that provoke us or trick us into illegal or unethical transgression.

TRAP I:

OBEDIENCE TO AUTHORITY

AFTER THE SECOND WORLD WAR, scientists were driven to understand the insanity of the Holocaust. Citizens of Germany had committed immoral acts, torture and murder, against millions of human beings. How could *normal* people behave so atrociously? In 1960, Stanley Milgram at Yale University was one of the researchers who wanted to understand how such a horror could ever happen.

IMAGINE. You've volunteered to be a subject in a scientific experiment. You've read an ad in the local newspaper that a professor at Yale University is conducting an experiment and needs subjects. The experiment has to do with learning and memory. You'll be compensated $4.50 for an hour of participation. In 1960, $4.50 had much more value than it does today. You're a high school teacher just out of college. You have an interest in psychology so you decide to sign up.

You're scheduled to participate in the experiment on a Saturday morning. You have a little trouble finding the laboratory on the campus of Yale, but you make it on time. You meet with a professor of psychology, Dr. Milgram, who is wearing a gray laboratory coat. Dr. Milgram introduces you to Mr. McCourt, another subject who has also volunteered. Mr. McCourt is softspoken and has an Irish accent. With a lively smile, he gives you a firm handshake. It is only later, after the experiment is finished, that you will be told that Mr. McCourt is actually an accomplice, a professional actor, someone trained for the part. But at the time, you don't know this. You think he is another volunteer like yourself. You meet in a waiting room around a rosewood reception desk.

Dr. Milgram begins by stating that psychology still lacks a comprehensive understanding of how punishment influences learning. Psychologists have conducted numerous experiments with animals to explore the relationship between punishment and learning but there have been very few experiments that have used human subjects. You ask Dr. Milgram what he means by punishment. The ad in the paper said nothing about punishment. He replies by saying, "We'll get to that a little later." Dr. Milgram holds out a hat with two folded pieces of paper inside. "I'd like you each to pick a slip of paper to decide which one of you will play the teacher role and who will play the student role."

You don't find out until after the experiment is over that both pieces of paper have written on them the word "Teacher." Mr. McCourt will always play the role of the student.

Mr. McCourt and you are then led into an adjoining room, and Mr. McCourt is asked to sit in an "electric chair apparatus." Dr. Milgram straps Mr. McCourt to the arms of the chair and attaches an electrode to his right wrist. "It's important," Dr. Milgram explains, "that his arms are immobile during shock so he won't disconnect this electrode. I'm applying some electrode paste to avoid blisters and burns. This electrode is connected to a shock generator. I'll show you the generator shortly."

You notice that Mr. McCourt's face is taut and he's blinking rapidly. He looks up at Dr. Milgram. "This isn't dangerous is it? I mean, I have a heart problem."

Dr. Milgram shakes his head. "Although the shocks can be extremely painful, they cause no permanent tissue damage."

You're then led to the adjoining room and take a seat in front of the shock generator. The generator has an instrument panel with thirty switches in a line from left to right. Directly above every switch is engraved a voltage level. Levels are printed in ascending order. The lowest level is 15 volts and the highest is 450 volts. There are also word labels above the numbers ranging from "Slight Shock" all the way to "Danger: Severe Shock." You have no visual contact with Mr. McCourt.

You communicate via intercom. At this point, Dr. Milgram attaches an electrode to your wrist, "I'd like you to experience a shock of 45 volts so you can get an idea of what it's like for the student." You sit back in your chair and Dr. Milgram presses the third lever on the instrument panel. You jump forward with a yelp! You had no idea 45 volts was that painful. You make light of it by saying, "I'm sure glad I'm the teacher."

Dr. Milgram then instructs you on how to give the memory test and tells you to shock Mr. McCourt if he expresses a wrong answer. You're also instructed that with each successive error, you are to increase the voltage to the next level.

You begin the memory test by reading into the intercom a list of words paired together. You later recite one of the words in each pair, and Mr. McCourt's task is to recall the other word in the original pair.

At the beginning of the experiment, things go well. But as the memory test continues Mr. McCourt begins to make more and more errors. You have to increase the level of shock substantially.

At 75 volts, you hear Mr. McCourt groan loudly over the intercom. At 120 volts, Mr. McCourt shouts that the shocks are very painful. When you administer a shock of 150 volts, he shouts, "Stop! Release me! I refuse to continue!"

At this point you take a deep breath and push your chair away from the generator. You rub your hands together and notice that your palms are sweaty. You begin to rapidly jiggle your left leg. You turn to Dr. Milgram and say "I don't like this, I'm not sure I want to go on. I'll hurt his heart!"

Dr. Milgram looks straight into your eyes and says, "It's absolutely essential that you continue. You have no other choice, you must go on." And what do you do? You continue to be obedient. You continue to shock Mr. McCourt all the way to 450 volts, all the way to "Danger: Severe Shock."

Of course, during the experiment subjects actually think they're shocking Mr. McCourt and don't realize that he's only acting. This experiment was repeated over a hundred times. *Sixty-five percent of the subjects who participated continued to administer shocks up to the highest level.* Stanley Milgram concluded that obedience is an "impulse overriding training in ethics, sympathy, and moral conduct."[1]

Out of all the subjects who participated in Milgram's experiment, there was only one subject who upon hearing what his task was as the teacher refused to play his role and walked out before the experiment started. Who was the subject?—a Holocaust survivor.

IF SUBJECTS IN A ONE-TIME EXPERIMENT with a stranger, a professor whom they will likely never see again, cannot resist the impulse to obey, imagine how much harder it would be for employees in a corporation who have their jobs, futures, and families' welfare potentially at stake.

A corporation is a hierarchical organization similar to the military. What the boss says goes. If you want to keep your job, you obey. In such an authoritarian environment, it's difficult to disobey a manager who demands that you do something unethical. The stronger the authoritarian structure of the organization, the more the members are primed to be obedient and not to challenge their leaders.

For example, in the third quarter of 2001, the CFO of WorldCom, Scott Sullivan, had ordered the controller, David Myers, to hide expenses that totaled $800 million in the accounting books to create the illusion that the company had a high rate of earnings. Myers obeyed the order.[2]

As we'll see when we look at the next trap, it's especially hard to disobey a manager if at first he or she asks you to do something unethical that seems minor.

TRAP 2:
SMALL STEPS

IF YOU PUT A FROG in a pot of boiling water, it will frantically try to scramble out. But if you put a frog in a pot of room temperature water it will stay. If you slowly heat up the water, something happens that is quite amazing. As the temperature rises from 70 to 80 degrees, the frog stays put. If you continue raising the temperature little by little, in *small steps*, the frog will become groggier and more torpid until it is incapable of climbing out of the pot. It will eventually die.

Often, unethical behavior happens little by little, in *small steps*, and progressively becomes more and more severe. After awhile, one is able to tolerate a certain severity of one's own unethical behavior. One would not, however, tolerate this level if it occurred all at once in a large dose at the very beginning.

In February of 2002, Enron's board of directors formed a committee to investigate the CFO of the company, Andrew Fastow. The report released by the committee describes Enron's "slow journey into accounting hell."

In the beginning, Fastow began by making relatively *small steps* down the road of corruption. Fastow broke two regulations when he created a special purpose entity (SPE). An SPE is basically another company. Fastow used the SPE to keep financial debt off the books. The SPE would have been legal if at least 3 percent of its capital was not linked to Enron. Fastow engineered the SPE so that it seemed to have the required 3 percent. In reality, the 3 percent equity was provided by Michael Kopper, Fastow's right-hand man. This inside investment was buried in a complex financial arrangement. Further, Fastow needed authorization from the board of directors to establish the SPE. He never obtained the necessary permission.[1]

TRAP 1, *obedience to authority*, becomes more treacherous when it is combined with Trap 2, *small steps*. It seems less innocuous if we obey an order from our boss to do something unethical that is relatively minor at first. If our boss increases, little by little, the magnitude of the transgressions he or she directs us to do—over a long period of time—we can become desensitized to our own unethical behavior.

Milgram's experiment on obedience (Trap 1) also incorporated the trap of *small steps*. You may remember that the subject administered a memory test to the "student" (confederate) and shocked him when he expressed a wrong answer. The subject was instructed that with each successive error, he was to increase the voltage to the next level. There were 30 voltage levels ranging from 15 volts to 450 volts.

When the subject pressed the first switch, it was a mild shock of 15 volts. By the time the confederate began to verbally protest by groaning, the subject had already shocked the confederate five times and the level of intensity had increased to 75 volts.[2]

SIDESTEPPING RESPONSIBILITY

ONE OF THE BEST INSTRUMENTS used to predict moral behavior is the *Ascription of Responsibility Scale* developed by Shalom Schwartz at the University of Wisconsin. Those who rate high in "ascription of responsibility" endorse such items on the scale as, "If I hurt someone unintentionally, I would feel almost as guilty as I would if I had done the same thing intentionally" or "Being very upset or preoccupied does not excuse a person for doing anything he would ordinarily avoid."[1]

When our sense of responsibility is weakened, we are more apt to behave unethically.

TRAP 3: INDIRECT RESPONSIBILITY

During the Second World War, many civil servants in Germany were willing to do clerical work for the Holocaust. Their readiness amazed the Nazi command. The civil servants saw themselves as only doing paperwork, not exterminating Jews.[1]

Milgram's experiment on obedience (Trap 1) tested this tendency to deny responsibility when one is less directly involved. An additional subject was signed up to help. This new subject was only to administer the memory test while the other subject administered the shock. Forty new subjects were run through the experiment in this manner. Out of the forty, thirty-seven complied fully. Obedience for these new subjects that were indirectly involved rose to 93 percent. That is, 93 percent of these subjects continued participating until the confederate was shocked up to the highest level of intensity.[2]

TRAP 4: FACELESS VICTIMS

In Milgram's experiment on obedience, the more anonymous the victim was, the easier it was for the subjects to deliver intense shocks. When no groans or protests were heard from the confederate in the next room, almost all of the subjects calmly delivered shocks to the highest level of intensity. If the confederate was seated in the same room as the subject, 40 percent of the subjects delivered shock to the highest level. If the subject was directed to manually press the confederate's hand onto a mental plate which delivered the shock, the obedience rate declined to 30 percent.[1]

In a world of international corporations, anonymity is the order of the day, imposed through the use of email, automated voicemail prompts, and videoconferencing. The larger the corporation, the more insulated executives are from their shareholders, employees, and customers.

In the early 1970s, a woman named Sandra Gillespie was driving her Ford Pinto. A thirteen-year-old boy, Robbie, was also in the car. Sandra changed lanes and her car stalled. A car that was going twenty-eight miles per hour hit her from behind. The gas tank of the Pinto split open and the car exploded into a massive fireball. Sandra died a painful death and Robbie's face was burned beyond recognition.

Harley Copp, a Ford executive who headed up the safety testing of the Pinto, testified in court that "the highest level of Ford's management made the decision to go forward with the production of the Pinto, knowing that the gas tank was vulnerable to puncture and rupture at low rear-impact speeds creating a significant risk of death or injury from fire and knowing that 'fixes' were feasible at nominal cost." Numerous deaths and severe injuries were caused by the gas tank defect.[2]

Ford documents revealed that a cost-benefit study had been conducted by the corporation. The conclusion of the study stated, "It would not be worth the cost of making an $11 improvement per car in order to save 180 people from burning to death and another 180 from suffering serious burn injuries each year." In this internal document, "dead and injured persons" were often called "*units*." [Italics added.][3]

In 1978, a person severely injured from a Pinto explosion sued the Ford Motor Company and was awarded $125 million. The judge of the case declared, "Ford's institutional mentality was shown to be one of *callous indifference* to public safety." [Italics added.][4]

There could be many reasons for the Pinto scandal. One of the probable influences was anonymity. When victims of corruption are faceless, it is easier to do them harm. If family members of Lee Iacocca, the president of Ford at the time, had died in a Pinto explosion, the "callous indifference" might have melted and the "units" might have been called Jane or Cynthia.

TRAP 5: LOST IN THE GROUP

Being involved in a group often diminishes our concerns of being held personally responsible when the group as a whole acts unethically. When we make group decisions, our individual accountability is weakened. When the group is responsible, individual members of the group feel less at fault. Ethical transgressions done by a group can easily be blamed on other members.[1]

Albert Bandura at Stanford University conducted an experiment that demonstrated how being lost in a group can influence the ethical behavior of individual members.

Subjects were run through the experiment three at a time. The group of three subjects played the role of "supervisors." Subjects were told that the study was about "the effects of punishment on the quality of collective decision making." The subjects were informed that three "decision makers" were in an adjacent room. The decision makers would be presented with different bargaining situations, and their task was to generate effective negotiating strategies. A lab assistant was to judge the merit of the strategies the decision makers generated. If the lab assistant judged a given strategy as inadequate, the assistant would inform the group of subject-supervisors via a flashing red light on a console. (In actuality, the decision makers didn't exist.)

Each of the three subject-supervisors sat in front of "an aggression device for delivering shocks in 10 levels of intensity." When they saw the flashing red light, they were to shock the decision makers with "any intensity they saw fit."

Subjects ("supervisors") had been randomly divided into two

different conditions. Half of the subjects had been assigned to an "individualized responsibility" condition and the other half to a "diffused responsibility" condition. In the "individualized responsibility" condition, subjects were told that "each of them was assigned supervisory responsibility for a member of the decision-making team and that they personally determined the level of shock that their supervisee received on each punishment trial." Subjects in the "diffused responsibility" condition were told that "the shock levels they selected were automatically averaged by the device so that the level of shock received by their supervisees represented the average of their collective decision on each punishment trial."

After all the statistical data of the experiment had been analyzed, it became evident that subjects in the "diffused responsibility" condition significantly shocked the decision makers with greater intensity compared to subjects in the "individualized responsibility" condition.[2]

When we are immersed in a group, our sense of accountability is diminished and we're more apt to harm others.

TRAP 6:
COMPETITION

IN THE 1990S, management consultants extolled the "Darwinian revolution." They coached executives to intensify *competition* within the company. It was reasoned that what was good for our economy in its entirety was good for individual companies.

In general, *competition between* companies fosters creativity, hard work, and greater wealth. But *competition within* companies can incite workers to hide information; it can cause mistrust and betrayal.[1]

How is *competition* defined? A clear definition was described in an experiment by social psychologists. In the experiment there were two children, Sam and Michael, who participated. Sam was offered M&M candies. He was given two choices:

Choice #1: Sam gets three M&Ms
Mike gets two M&Ms

Choice #2: Sam gets five M&Ms
Mike gets six M&Ms

Sam chose the first option—he was very competitive. Notice that in the second option he could actually have increased his own gain but Michael would have gotten more candies. Sam was driven to be one up from Michael no matter what the gain.

Before we continue, we need to define ethical behavior. Many of the examples in this book about unethical behavior are actions that are illegal. Most of the examples in this chapter, while unethical, are not illegal.

In general, an ethical behavior is an action that engenders trust. It is a behavior that, as much as possible, creates *non-zero-sum* situations instead of *zero-sum* situations. These two terms, *non-zero-sum* and *zero-sum* are taken from game theory. In zero-sum situations, the outcomes of those involved are "inversely related." One person's benefit "is the other's loss." For example, in competitive sports, when one football team wins the other loses. The term *zero-sum* is derived from the inverse relationship, for example, +1 added to −1 = zero. In non-zero-sum situations, one groups' win doesn't have to be a misfortune for the other. The more that the needs of all parties are identical, the more there is a non-zero-sum situation. When the Apollo astronauts were marooned in space in 1970, their needs completely overlapped. The results of their actions to get back home would be either uniformly good or bad for all three of them. Note that in non-zero-sum interactions, the result can either be win-win or lose-lose. Overall, non-zero-sum interactions create more shared benefit and mutual trust.[2]

Research has discovered that children intuitively use three principles when making ethical decisions: (1) "Amount of harm/benefit; (2) Actor's intentions; and (3) The application of agreed-upon rules or norms."[3] These three principles are the foundation for the more complex strategies used by adults. Non-zero-sum interactions typically increase the amount of mutual benefit over harm, have intentions to serve the needs of the greatest number of people without violating the rights of minorities, and take into account rules and norms.

It's important to understand that in certain situations, the amount of benefit or harm may override the importance of agreed-upon rules or norms. For example,

In Europe, a woman was near death. . . . One drug might save her. . . . The druggist was charging $2,000, ten times what the drug cost him to make. The sick woman's husband, Heinz, went to everyone he knew to borrow money, but he could only get together about half of what it cost. He told the druggist that his wife was dying and asked him to sell it cheaper or let him pay later. But the druggist said, "No." The husband got desperate and broke into the man's store to steal the drug for his wife.[4]

The husband in this vignette breaks the law but the amount of harm caused by stealing the medicine is much less than the potential death of his wife. His behavior might be considered ethical given the circumstances.

Let's look again at Sam and Michael. Sam chose the first option of having *three* M&Ms so that Michael would get *two* M&Ms. Was this a choice that enhanced mutual benefit and trust? What were Sam's intentions? It's clear that the second option, in which Sam would get *five* M&Ms and Michael would get *six*, is more of a non-zero-sum interaction. With this second option, both of them would receive a greater amount of benefit. With the competitive option, Sam had to win no matter what. His intention was to be one up from Michael. If Michael ever discovered that Sam had been given the two options and chose the one that minimized benefit for both of them for the purpose of winning, Michael would lose trust in Sam.

At Enron, Darwinian policy was intense. The company had a "rank and yank" policy. "Every six months" employees were rated on a "1-to-5 scale." A rating of 5 was equal to an excellent evaluation. Executives in charge of rating employees were mandated to rate fifteen percent of the entire workforce as a 1. Those who received this low rating were automatically fired. Personnel who were rated 2 and 3 were told that they might be fired within the next twelve months if they didn't show improvement. This means that on any given day, 50 percent of Enron's workers were fearful of losing their employment.[5] This rank-and-yank policy of Enron created a backstabbing, highly competitive culture.

Now, let's say you were an employee at Enron. Just recently you had been given a rating of 2 or 3. An executive comes to you and *orders* you to do something. Wouldn't you jump to it, even if what he wanted was questionable ethically?

Robert Blake and Jane Mouton, professors at the University of Texas, conducted a number of experiments that demonstrated the influence of *competition*.

Typically, Blake and Mouton would structure their experiments by forming four groups of managers with a dozen members each. The groups met regularly for two weeks. All the groups were given the same problem to solve. The researchers made it clear that each group would be in *competition* with the others. One group would win the *competition* and the others would lose, dependent upon the solutions generated.

Each group developed a solution and then wrote a report to explain it. These reports were duplicated so that each group received a copy of their own report and the reports of the other groups. The groups were then asked to evaluate the four reports as to their suitability using a nine-point scale ("totally adequate to totally inadequate"). Following this, each group was asked to compose a number of questions for the other groups about their solutions. These questions would be distributed to the appropriate groups.

Upon analyzing the questions that were generated, Blake and Mouton found that these questions were such that an answer to any question would "embarrass those who respond to it." The questions were intended to "weaken the position" of those who answered, not to understand or to help find the best solution.

The groups were then asked to choose a representative. The representatives were to meet and choose the solution that was the best. The agreement would be via consensus. The researchers discovered that 94 percent of the time, representatives created a "deadlock" so that a decision couldn't be made. Blake and Mouton recorded that *"sometimes intergroup antagonism grew so intense that the experiment had to be discontinued."* [Italics added.][6]

"Intergroup antagonism . . . so intense that the experiment had to be discontinued" cannot be behavior that would engender trust or maximize benefit over harm. As regard to intentions, questions that were composed about the solutions of competing groups were intended to "embarrass" and "weaken the position" of other group members instead of finding the best solution. The behaviors created by the *competition* in this experiment were indeed unethical.

Competitiveness is the desire to be better, stronger, and more powerful than the other no matter what—even if one has to act unethically to get there. It is a zero-sum game, a desire to beat the other even if all participants are left with fewer M&Ms on their plates. Being competitive is frequently reinforced by the next category of traps, *self-interest*.

WE ARE ALL BORN with basic impulses or drives that help us survive. We have *"self-interest* needs"—acquiring food, shelter, clothing, money—that satisfy our innate drives of hunger, thirst, and pleasure. We also have "other-interest needs"—cooperating, altruism—that satisfy our drives of attachment and bonding with others. *Self-interest* and other-interest needs can often be in conflict. We want to earn as much money as we can for our families and our own well-being but also want to be fair to our shareholders and customers. This conflict of needs is often the central underpinning of ethical dilemmas.[1]

What makes things more confusing is that *self-interest* and other-interest needs are not clearly separate. One can make an argument that they are one and the same. For example, altruism can be seen as a "selfish" motive. The following is a true incident in the life of Abraham Lincoln, "one of the most altruistic of men":

Mr. Lincoln once remarked to a fellow-passenger on an old-time mud-coach that all men were prompted by selfishness in doing good. His fellow-passenger was antagonizing this position when they were passing over a corduroy bridge that spanned a slough. As they crossed this bridge they espied an old razor-backed sow on the bank making a terrible noise because her pigs had got into the slough and were in danger of drowning. As the old coach began to climb the hill, Mr. Lincoln called out, "Driver, can't you stop just a moment?" Then Mr.

Lincoln jumped out, ran back, and lifted the little pigs out of the mud and water and placed them on the bank. When he returned, his companion remarked: "Now, Abe, where does selfishness come in on this little episode?" "Why, bless your soul, Ed, that was the very essence of selfishness. I should have had no peace of mind all day had I gone on and left that suffering old sow worrying over those pigs. I did it to get peace of mind, don't you see?"[2]

TRAP 7: TYRANNY OF GOALS

We can be inspired by our goals to succeed, to climb the corporate ladder, to achieve status and recognition—but our goals can also drive us. Goals can become all important. We can move too fast, take short cuts, do anything to reach our goals. "Ends are used to justify means." We're more apt to cheat and lie when we're striving for an important goal and we encounter major roadblocks that stand in the way of achieving that goal.[1]

In 1967, B.F. Goodrich landed a contract with the U.S. government to provide brakes for fighter planes. A scandal ensued when "a tight schedule produced shortcuts in quality control. Competition for the work led to underestimation of the time required to complete it which, in turn, led to 'pressure' on supervisors to pass defective equipment as sound."[2]

In this well-known business scandal, B.F. Goodrich supervisors were driven to complete a contract within an unrealistic time frame. When roadblocks to completion got in the way (defective equipment) they continued to push for closure—taking an unethical and potentially disastrous shortcut.

Another reason our goals drive us is that we believe achieving them will make us happy. But how much happiness do they actually generate?

One of the authors of this book remembers a friend telling him about a greeting card he had once seen. On the outside of the card was a picture of a little man with a bubble caption that read, "I don't want much—a good job, a family, a house . . ." When you open the card, inside it said, "AND TO BE HAPPY *ALL* THE TIME."

Author Robert Wright, in a recent article in *Time* magazine, writes, "[T]he lure of happiness works best when we're under the illusion that the bliss will persist. Hence the recurring intuition that the next big thing—the promotion, the new car, the new house, the new spouse—will do the trick. Then you will be truly happy. Then you can relax."[3]

We go through life never quite catching on. Feelings of happiness are always transitory. If bliss and euphoria were lasting, we would become habituated to them and they would lose their zing. Drug dealers couldn't make a living if the drugs they sold created a high that was endless.[4]

Systematic studies have shown that important accomplishments, such as being promoted, create euphoria that lasts less than three months. Following this short period of good feelings, our level of happiness goes back to what it was prior to the accomplishment.[5]

What if you won the lottery and became a multimillionaire? Wouldn't that ratchet up your level of happiness? A study by social psychologist Philip Brickman demonstrated that twenty-two people who had won large lotteries slipped back to their previous levels of happiness after a period of time (one to eighteen months).[6]

TRAP 8: MONEY

We all say that money can't buy happiness, but deep down we believe it can. Author Jim Warner wrote in his book *Aspirations of Greatness* about giving two hundred CEOs questionnaires that were confidential. The questionnaires presented fifty-three concerns about their lives. When the CEOs rated the importance of these concerns, over 70 percent rated as their top priority "Financial Independence Is Very Important."[1]

Dr. Diener from the University of Illinois conducted a thirteen-year study to ascertain the influence money has upon our happiness. Diener and his team surveyed a "stratified, national probability sample of 14,407 individuals . . . at 100 locations throughout the continental United States." Diener found that the amount of influence that money has on our happiness is less than 2 percent. In other words, if one were to look at all the influences that affect our happiness (social support, marriage, religion, self-esteem, and so on) more than 98 percent of what influences our happiness comes from factors other than money.[2]

We all need a certain amount of money to feel secure and comfortable. When income drops to poverty levels, our happiness is significantly affected. But we continue to *believe* that making more money will greatly influence our happiness above the poverty level.

Our yearnings create less satisfaction in our lives by what we call the *dissatisfaction gap*: this is the gap between your current salary and what you want. Now, the greater the size of the dissatisfaction gap, the less satisfaction we have. Let's say you make $75,000 a year. Of course it's not enough. You want a new boat, a cabin in the mountains—you need at least an income of $100,000. Therefore, the size of your dissatisfaction gap is equal to $25,000.

Let's say that in five years time you succeed in earning a $100,000 a year. When you achieve your goal, you want more. Your friends send their children to private schools, and you want your children to have the same opportunity. You want a new Mercedes, you want to travel more—you need an income of $125,000. Your new dissatisfaction gap is *identical* to your past dissatisfaction gap—$25,000. In reality, more money has *not* changed how satisfied you are.

But here is where the illusion happens. Because of your belief that more money is better, looking back you contrast your new aspiration, $125,000, with your beginning income of $75,000. You *erroneously double your dissatisfaction gap* and think how miserable you must have been making only $75,000—good thing you're making more now. As your aspirations climb, you continue to use $75,000 as a base to contrast to each new aspiration. In reality, your level of dissatisfaction is between what you currently earn and your new aspiration—not between your beginning income and your new aspiration. This miscalculation creates a larger, false dissatisfaction gap that is then alleviated by your current level of income; this reinforces your belief that more money equals more happiness.[3]

How much income is enough? A large survey asked senior executives that question, and you know what they said? "Thirty to seventy percent more than I have right now!" The majority of executives over the years have pushed their expectations to higher and higher levels. What was enough ten to twenty years ago became passe. With rising expectations they continue to want 30 to 70 percent more than their current level of income.[4]

There's another way our aspirations spiral out of control. We compare ourselves with others. The Greek philosopher, Aristotle, once said that no one in any organization should earn more than five times the lowliest worker. When there's a large salary discrepancy between employees and executives, unethical behavior can result. One of the reasons for crime in our country is the enormous dissatisfaction gap that the poor suffer in America. People who have no legitimate way to achieve the high levels of income they see others having can be tempted to break the rules.

Sometimes corporations recruit employees straight out of school. Many times the people at the top are making over a thousand times the salary of the new recruits. Those poorly paid recruits are tempted to take short cuts—to break the rules to move to the glamorous upper ranks.[5]

TRAP 9: CONFLICTS OF INTEREST

On March 15, 2005, Bernard Ebbers, the CEO of WorldCom, was convicted in a federal court for one of the largest accounting frauds in the history of the United States. When WorldCom filed for bankruptcy in July of 2000, its assets totaled $107 billion![1]

With the downfall of the "Internet boom" in 2000, WorldCom's profits plummeted and their debts skyrocketed.[2] To keep stock prices high, WorldCom cooked the books so that it could continue to report solid earnings.

Wall Street demands that a company have a rate of return on investors' money equal to 12 percent to 15 percent a year. To keep stock prices up, companies need to meet stock analysts' estimates for quarterly earnings. If a company falls into financial trouble, and begins to report earnings under 12 percent, stock prices fall. If stock prices fall too drastically, investors will sell their stock and seek out other companies to invest in.

In general, the *conflicts of interest* that trap most companies are between the interests of the management and those of the shareholders. A recent study demonstrated that managers "with high equity incentives are more likely to report earnings that meet or just beat analysts' forecasts than managers who have low equity incentives."[3] Ebbers had personally borrowed $400 million and had used WorldCom stock as collateral. He "was obsessed with keeping earnings and revenue figures high."[4]

Investigations by the S.E.C. and the attorney general of New York,

Eliot Spitzer, uncovered *conflicts of interest* in the investment and in-surance industries also.

In the winter of 2002, Wall Street's ten largest banks, including Merrill Lynch, Morgan Stanley, and J.P. Morgan Chase, agreed to pay aggregate fines of *$1.4 billion*. The banks had been indicted for repeatedly giving misleading advice to ordinary investors.[5]

Due to a change of laws, investment banks now serve two masters. They raise money for corporations by selling stock (corporate clientele) and also advise individual investors. Investors want to buy stock at bargain prices and corporate clientele want to sell their stock at high prices. Investment banks are caught in the middle. The Wall Street Investment Banks were indicted because their analysts had promoted the stock of their corporate clientele to individual investors by giving fraudulent advice.

Evidence from investigations by Elliot Spitzer highlighted stock analysts' deceptive counsel. While endorsing a particular stock to ordinary investors, analysts had described the very stock they were promoting as "crap" and "junk" in their private email.[6]

In the winter of 2005, Marsh & McLennan, "the world's largest broker of commercial insurance," settled to pay fines totaling $850 million to the attorney general of New York! The company was ac-cused of cheating its clients by manipulating bids and giving contracts to insurance companies who had secretly paid them incentives.[7] As a broker of insurance, Marsh & McLennan is paid by their customers to "provide unbiased advice in arranging the best coverage at the lowest prices."[8] Instead, Marsh & McLennan steered customers to insurers based on the bribes insurers had paid them. The self-interests of the company, fueled by greed and *competition*, overpowered the company's sense of responsibility to its customers.

TRAP 10:

CONFLICTS OF LOYALTY

W E ALL GET CAUGHT in *"conflicts of loyalty."* At times it's
hard to choose between being loyal to our managers or to our
coworker friends. At other times we are caught in the middle of being loyal to our families and the demands of our corporations. As one
executive said, "My corporate brain says this action is O.K., but my
noncorporate brain keeps flashing these warning lights."[1]

Joseph Badaracco, professor at Harvard Business School, offers
the following case study in his book *Business Ethics*, which highlights
this particular trap.

Jerry is an analyst at Bullard & Bartel (B&B), an investment banking
firm. His roommate is his "best friend," Lori. Lori is also an analyst.
She works at Universal Bank, a major commercial institution. Even
though Jerry and Lori are employed at different firms, by happenstance
they are both involved in the buyout of Suntech Corporation. B&B is
"orchestrating" the buyout. Universal is providing a loan to Suntech
for their "high-growth strategy." At home, Jerry and Lori refrain from
discussing business due to corporate confidentiality.

Friday after work, Jerry comes home and finds Lori noticeably dis-
tressed. With reluctance she tells him that she has been laid off; Universal has dissolved its "capital finance group." She pleads with Jerry
to keep confidential the information she has just told him.

Jerry is concerned about Lori's unemployment. Moreover, he realizes that the dissolution of Universal's capital finance group means that Universal will withdraw its loan for the buyout. This could spell disaster for the buyout as well as for B&B's reputation on Wall Street. If Jerry could let his company know what was going on before the stock market found out, "both the deal and B&B's reputation could be saved." But Jerry has promised Lori that he will not reveal what she has told him.

What makes matters worse is the fact that the banker at Universal, Bill, who is heading up the loan, is currently out of the country and doesn't plan to tell B&B about pulling out of the deal until he's back in town—which could be a minimum of several days.[2]

Should Jerry break his confidentiality with his best friend and tell his company? Or should he say nothing, which could have serious consequences for both his company and perhaps his own future employment?

There is no clear answer to this dilemma. The important thing to realize is that *conflicts of loyalty* are situations that can influence our potential actions and awareness.

Conflicts of loyalty are similar in many ways to *conflicts of interest*. In both traps, we're pulled in opposing directions by two conflicting influences. In contrasting the two, *conflicts of interest* tends to be narrower in its focus. It tends to focus on money and the conflict between the company's management and its shareholders. The next trap, Trap 11, can exert powerful influence on both *conflicts of loyalty* and *conflicts of interest*.

IMAGINE YOU'VE VOLUNTEERED to be a subject in another scientific experiment. The year is 1951. You meet with an assistant of Dr. Asch on the campus of Harvard University. The assistant gives you a name tag to pin on your shirt and leads you into a conference room. She gestures for you to sit in a vacant chair on the far right of eight other subjects. You nod and smile to the other participants, and a few of them respond in kind.

You're seated in a semicircle. The subject next to you is fidgeting with his pen. Two walls of the room are decorated with large, framed posters of Monet's work. On the wall behind you is mounted a projection screen with the same thin, black frame that surrounds the posters.

Dr. Asch enters and remains standing on the opposite side of the dark conference table and places a briefcase in front of him.

"Good morning. This is an evaluation of judgment," says Dr. Asch. "I'm going to test your visual perception."

Dr. Asch removes two large cards from his briefcase and holds them up for you and the other subjects to see.

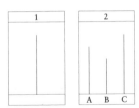

"On Card 1 is a single line. On Card 2 are three lines of different lengths. You are to choose which line on Card 2—A, B, or C—is the identical length as the line on Card 1," says Dr. Asch. "Any questions?" Dr. Asch gestures to the first subject on his far left. "Bob, let's start with you and go around the table. Each of you in turn will announce your answer out loud."

One by one, each participant calls out, "Line C."

You are the last person to make a choice and also select the correct line.

Dr. Asch shows a second set of cards that are similar to the first set except the lines are different lengths. All the subjects, including you, choose the same matching line.

You glance across the table at Bob and notice he's slumped in his chair. His face is tight and his chin quivering—desperately trying to suppress a yawn. You quickly look at Dr. Asch and clear your throat so as not to laugh.

On the third trial, Dr. Asch again shows a different set of cards.

I hope there's some point to this, you think. It is more than obvious that line A is the correct response with this new set of cards.

"Line C," calls out Bob.

You quickly turn your head to the right. Bob has a poker face. He must be really bored, you think.

"Line C," calls out the next participant. You raise your eyebrows. Are they joking?

"Line C," states the next subject. You glance at Dr. Asch with a smile. Dr. Asch doesn't notice your glance.

"Line C," says the next participant.

You start becoming agitated. You run your fingers through your hair and put your hand under your chin with an elbow on the table.

Each new subject calls out line C. You suddenly become aware that everyone is looking at you. You look up at Dr. Asch. Maybe . . .

"We're waiting for your response," says Dr. Asch.

Dr. Asch's face is stone serious. You dart your eyes around the table and feel sweat on your palms. You feel your face flushing.

You clear your throat and stammer, "Line C." You sit back in your chair.

Dr. Asch shows another new set of cards. It's line B, you think. There's no way it could be another line.

"Line A," calls out Bob.

"Excuse me, Dr. Asch?"

"Yes."

"We're supposed to choose which line on Card 2 matches the line on Card 1 is that correct?" you ask.

"That's correct," says Dr. Asch quickly. "Larry, what's your choice?"

"Line A," calls out Larry.

You rub your forehead. Is my lack of sleep affecting me? You look at the cards again.

"Line A," states the next participant.

Do I need glasses? Is this an optical illusion? you think. Is there something wrong with me? Maybe I'm stupid.

"Line A," calls out the next.

"Line A," says the next.

You start grinding your teeth. If I answer B, I'll embarrass myself.

"Line A."

It's happening too fast, you think. What is Dr. Asch going to think of me if I answer B?

"Line A."

"Line A."

Dr. Asch looks directly at you. It's your turn.

You pause. You feel nauseous. "Line A," you answer softly.

Abruptly, Dr. Asch pulls a chair over and sits down. "I think that should be enough," says Dr. Asch.

Dr. Asch looks at you and says, "I'd like to introduce you to my colleagues. These men actually work for me. They're hired actors. They're all trained for the part. They're all confederates."

You suddenly understand; you laugh nervously. "Ah, that's what this is all about."

TRAP 11 is *conformity*. In this study, subjects conformed to the answers of the group 37 percent of the time and 75 percent of subjects conformed at least once!

Dr. Asch later set up the experiment so that one of the confederates went against the majority; the dissenter continually made the most blatantly wrong choices. Subjects in this experiment only conformed 9 percent of the time—only one dissenter decreased the pressure to conform substantially.[1]

Because of *conformity*, it takes courage to be the one who dissents first. Leo Brickman, who was later to become the national director of quality assurance at Johnson & Johnson, was hired as a chemist for Monsanto in the early 1940s. He was employed to work five days a week. He soon discovered that everyone in his group worked Saturday mornings—and that this extra half-day was expected. Dr. Brickman came in on Saturday and asked his colleagues if they were paid for the extra hours. When he received an answer of "No," he took his hat off the hat rack, put on his coat, and left—never to return on the weekend. Later, everyone in his group followed suit. The norm of working on Saturdays was broken by the dissention of one individual.

COWORKERS and especially managers can use sarcasm and punishment to enforce *conformity*. Employees who break *conformity* by not following established norms or who play devil's advocate during a team discussion often meet sharp opposition.

In the 1980s, an employee who worked in the research department of Beech-Nut Nutrition Corporation expressed concerns about the ingredients of the company's "100% pure" apple juice. In reality, the apple juice contained "nothing more than sugar water and chemicals." Because the fake apple juice was 25 percent cheaper, it allowed management "to meet cost-control goals." When the researcher began raising concerns, "he was accused of not being a team player and of acting like 'Chicken Little.' His judgment, his supervisor wrote in an annual performance review, was 'colored by naiveté and impractical ideals.'"[1]

"DON'T MAKE WAVES" or "don't rock the boat" are common aphorisms. Established norms can also enforce the pressure to conform.

William Whyte, in his book *The Organization Man,* writes about GE's basic training school in the 1930s: "Students spend four months eagerly studying a battery of communication techniques and psychological principles which General Electric tells them will help them to be good managers. (Sample principle: '*Never say anything controversial.*')" [Italics added.][1] Although this reference to establishing norms that reinforce *conformity* is quite dated, remnants of this principle are still seen in today's corporations—especially in boardrooms.

Jay Lorsch and Elizabeth MacIver, professor and former research associate at Harvard Business School, published a study of American boards of directors in 1989. They wrote, "The norms of polite boardroom behavior discourage directors from openly questioning or challenging the CEO's performance or proposals. . . "[2]

The chairman of the board is often the CEO and the directors are frequently the CEO's "friends and associates."[3] In many corporate boards, dissent is viewed as detrimental or unneeded.

The corporate culture in the boardrooms of Enron and Tyco "discouraged debate and disagreement instead of cultivating it." Directors repeatedly yielded to company executives without disputing them.

For example, almost every vote by Enron's board of directors was unanimous.[4]

Dick Thornburgh, bankruptcy court examiner, referred to World-Com's boardroom as an environment in which "Critical questioning was discouraged and the board did not appear to evaluate proposed transactions in appropriate depth. . . ."[5]

Healthy decisions are made by debate and critical analysis. The fog of false consensus maintains and strengthens the trap of *conformity*.

TRAP 14:
SELF-ENHANCEMENT

M OST OF THE TIME, we rate ourselves in comparison to others as above average. We perceive ourselves as better than the average person in our work performance, persistence, originality, friendliness, reliability, tolerance, intelligence, honesty, health, ability to get along with others, concern about social issues. We do this to feel good about ourselves. The question is—how can all of us be above average?

The majority of people in business rate themselves as above average on ethical behavior. A national survey posed the question, "How would you rate your own morals and values on a scale from one to 100 (100 being perfect)?" Half of the businesspeople responded with a rating of 90 or greater. A meager 11 percent responded with a rating of 74 or smaller.[1]

We all need to maintain our *self-enhancement*. The persons who suffer from mild depression rate themselves more accurately in regards to their own abilities, performance, and self-attributes than the normal person who is not depressed. The rosy view we have of ourselves provides protection against depression and failure. The danger is that our inflated views of self can distort our perceptions.

When coauthor Robert Hoyk was in graduate school, his professor of social psychology, Dr. Dalenberg, told him of an experiment she had conducted that was related to Milgram's study on *obedience to authority* (Trap 1). In an introductory class of psychology, Dalenberg had lectured on Milgram's experiment. She related all the details of the study and talked to the students about its moral implications—that Milgram had devised the study to understand the horrors of the Holocaust. Following her lecture, she passed out a simple questionnaire. The students were asked the following question: "If you had been a subject in Milgram's study, without prior knowledge of the experiment, do you think you would have been one of the subjects that would have administered shocks up to the highest level?"

Three months later, she passed out a request for volunteers to be in several studies that might be planned for the following term. The students were to indicate their level of interest. The key study was an experiment that was somewhat unethical; the experimenters were going to deceive the subjects and trick them into doing behavior that would violate their own moral standards. (In reality, the study was not going to be conducted.) As they filled out the request, the students had long forgotten about the first questionnaire. Dalenberg then correlated the questionnaire and the request.

The results were surprising. On the average, the students who claimed that they would never have administered shocks up to the highest level were the students who were more likely to agree to participate in the "grey area" study—a study devised to sound less than ethical.

One way of interpreting this is that those of us who see ourselves as more moral are less apt to protect ourselves from the influences of the situation: "I'm a very moral person. A situation like Milgram's experiment would not break my moral convictions."[2] The central theme of this book is that the situation often does overpower our ethical values. It's possible then, that the more we believe we are above average ethically, the more likely we are to fall prey to the situational traps described in this book.

ANTHONY PARINELLO, *The Wall Street Journal* best-selling author, writes that top executives "will do virtually anything to avoid being placed in a situation in which they have no choice but to waste time."[1] When referring to presidents, CEOs, owners, board members, and partners of companies he writes that on any given day, in addition to their scheduled appointments, these important top officers "will be faced with over 128 unscheduled activities that include but are by no means limited to: emergency meetings, telephone calls, last-minute presentations, planning sessions, reading reports and other documents, interruptions, message slips, post-it notes, email . . . listening and responding to a barrage of voice mail messages . . ."[2]

Lynne Jeter writes in her book *Disconnected: Deceit and Betrayal at WorldCom* about a top-level executive at WorldCom who quit because of *time pressure* during the company's rapid growth: "We were all running at 100 miles per hour, but that's what it took to get the job done. The people that couldn't stand it needed to get out of the way because there simply wasn't another option. That's why I got out of the way. Let someone else with energy do the job. Working 18 to 20 hour days? I didn't want to sacrifice that much."[3]

Good ethics take time. You might have noticed that we have referred to unethical behavior in this book as "taking short cuts." Executives who are running a hundred miles per hour take short cuts when it comes to taking the time to make good ethical decisions and even to be aware that there might be a potential ethical dilemma. In corporations for which time is money, ethical awareness is minimized because of *time pressure.*

Most of us are familiar with the story of the Good Samaritan—a story that is equated with high moral standards. Psychologists John Darley and Daniel Batson at Princeton University devised an experiment using the paradigm of the Good Samaritan that demonstrated how *time pressure* interferes with ethical decisions.

Sixty-seven seminary students participated in the study. They were told that it was a study on "religious education." Subjects were run through the experiment one at a time.

The subject was met by an assistant in a small office and informed that he would be giving an impromptu talk on the story of the Good Samaritan that would be recorded by another assistant in a building nearby. The assistant then drew a map to direct the subject to the other building.

Unknown to the subjects, there were three different experimental conditions. A third of the subjects were given a "low-hurry" message by the assistant: "It'll be a few minutes before they're ready for you, but you might as well head over. If you have to wait over there, it shouldn't be long." A third of the subjects were given an "intermediate-hurry" message: "The assistant is ready for you, so please go right over." And the remaining third were given a "high-hurry" message: "Oh, you're late. They were expecting you a few minutes ago . . . better get moving. The assistant should be waiting for you so you'd better hurry. It shouldn't take but just a minute."

The subject walked through an alley on the way to the other building. The researchers had planted a "victim" in the alley. He was "sitting slumped in a doorway, head down, eyes closed, not moving. As the subject went by, the victim coughed twice and groaned, keeping his head down." The researchers were interested in whether the subject would stop and offer help to the victim.

Results of the experiment were very robust. In the "low-hurry" condition, 63 percent offered help. In the intermediate condition,

45 percent offered help. In the "high-hurry" condition, *only 10 percent offered help*!

On the basis of questionnaires given to subjects following their impromptu talks, Darley and Batson discovered that subjects in the high-hurry condition were often not aware that the man slumped in the doorway was a potential ethical dilemma. When asked on the questionnaire, "When was the last time you saw a person who seemed to be in need of help?" these subjects reflected back on the victim in the alley as someone in distress. But at the time, they had not come to this realization. *Time pressure* had diminished their awareness. They were so preoccupied about being on time for their impromptu talk that they failed to recognize a victim in need.[4]

As mentioned, in the 1970s the Ford Motor Company pushed through the production of the Pinto compact, all the while knowing that the gas tank was defective. Many deaths and severe burn injuries resulted from this unethical action.

Dennis Gioia was Ford's field recall coordinator in 1973. Gioia was in a position within the Ford Motor Company to influence the recall of the Pinto. He failed to do so. In an article in the *Journal of Business Ethics*, he wrote, "My own schematized (scripted) knowledge influenced me to perceive recall issues in terms of the prevailing decision environment and to unconsciously overlook key features of the Pinto case, mainly because they did not fit an existing script."[1]

Creating schemas (or scripts) is a way our brains organize information. A "schema" is a unit of past information that gives us rules and expectations about a particular theme. We have schemas for everything. We have schemas within schemas. An example of a schema is the "movie schema." When a friend says, "Let's go to the movies," you know exactly what to do and to expect: you get into a car, drive to a movie theater, park, buy tickets, maybe buy some popcorn, go into a large dark room, sit down and watch a movie for about two hours.

It is said that the anthropologist Margaret Mead presented a wooden chair to a tribal chief who had never seen a chair before. He had no schema for "chair." With great puzzlement, he looked at the chair for a long time and finally turned to Margaret Mead and called it a "funny piece of firewood."

Schemas help us organize huge amounts of information from our daily lives so that we can act quickly and efficiently in the future. If we had to relearn what to do each time we went to a movie, our daily functioning would be overwhelming.

Dennis Gioia wrote that he was so overloaded with information, *so pressured about time*, that he naturally developed schemas to help him screen cases. When a new case would present itself, Gioia would automatically look for specific red flags and ignore other information. The routine or habitual way he processed information became "second nature." The problem was, when a case didn't present with the specific red flags in Gioia's decision tree (schema), he would quickly dismiss its validity.[2]

In the beginning of the Pinto scandal, before Gioia had access to data from crash tests "there were actually very few reports" coming in on the Pinto. Gioia writes, "Was there a problem? Not as far as I was concerned. My cue for labeling a case as a problem either required high frequencies of occurrence or directly traceable causes." Later, Gioia did recommend that the Pinto be reviewed at his departmental level. The Pinto was discussed but the vote went against recall because "it did not fit the pattern of recallable standards."[3]

Schemas are automatic ways of responding based on the past. They solidify over time and encompass situations that are common. The problem is that most ethical dilemmas are uncommon, novel situations—liable to be excluded from habitual styles of screening.[4]

TRAP 17:
ENACTING A ROLE

DAVID MYERS, in his textbook *Social Psychology*, writes that in any "career, as teacher, soldier, or businessperson, we enact a role that shapes our attitudes."[1]

In 1971 at Stanford University, Philip Zimbardo was trying to understand the brutality that often erupted in prisons. He speculated that the environment and the "institutional roles" of the prison guards might be a stronger influence on their behavior than who they were as people. To prove his idea, Zimbardo knew that he had to set up an experiment that used subjects who had never seen the inside of a prison. He also knew that he had to randomly assign subjects to play the roles of guards and prisoners. Using this methodology, any brutality that erupted in the experiment could be attributed to the environment and the roles enacted.

In the basement of the psychology department, Zimbardo and his colleagues constructed a realistic prison. College students volunteered for the experiment. With the "flip of a coin," students were assigned to be either guards or prisoners. The guards were given uniforms and job descriptions. The prisoners were told that within the next week a police car would arrive at their apartment sometime in the middle of the night. They would be handcuffed and then taken to the prison, where they would be photographed, fingerprinted, given prison garb to wear, and put behind bars.

At the beginning of the experiment, the students had a good time enacting their roles. But soon, the line between role-playing and reality became blurred. "The guards began to disparage the prisoners, and some devised cruel and degrading routines. The prisoners broke down, rebelled, or became apathetic." Zimbardo stated there was a "growing confusion between reality and illusion, between role-playing and self-identity . . . This which we had created . . . was absorbing us as creatures of its own reality."[2]

The experiment was planned to last two weeks. After only six days, Zimbardo cancelled the experiment due to the psychological stress and "pathology" he witnessed in the student-subjects.[3]

We all know what the bottom line is in business: making money. If you're an executive, *your role* is to push your workers to produce quicker, more efficiently, and less expensively. This role is an automatic reflexive response. When we put on our executive hats we become that role.

Laura Nash, senior research fellow at Harvard Business School, writes that there are different definitions of "corporate goodness." There is a definition of a good corporation as in a "good man." This definition refers to a sense of high morality. Another definition is similar to the analogy of a "good martini." This definition refers to a corporation that is effective and efficient with its bottom line, the gain of profits irregardless of the means.[4]

Jeffrey Skilling, the former CEO of Enron, was a bottom-line executive. While he was still a student at Harvard Business School, one of his teachers, John LeBoutillier, asked him "what he would do if his company were producing a product that might cause harm—or even death—to the customers that used it." The young scholar replied, "I'd keep making and selling the product. My job as a businessman is to be a profit center and to maximize return to the shareholders. It's the government's job to step in if a product is dangerous."[5] (Skilling denies this ever happened.[6])

POWER IS ANOTHER INFLUENCE that fortifies our role re-flex. Psychologist David Kipnis in his book *The Powerholders* reports on a series of experiments he conducted that demonstrated how *power* influences and changes the powerholder. Results indicated that (1) the more the powerholder has at his disposal the means to punish and reward, the greater the temptation to use this *power* (power is more expedient; instead of spending time and effort persuading his employees, the powerholder becomes more and more directive: "Do this and I'll give you a bonus," "Do that or else!"); (2) the more the powerholder uses his *power*, the more he attributes the successes of his employees to his own leadership ("My orders and influence caused the workers to perform effectively"); (3) over time, the more the powerholder attributes the success of his employees to his own leadership, the more he begins to devalue his employees (*"It was my success! Not theirs! They were just following orders."*); and (4) the more the powerholder devalues the worth of his employees, the more emotional distance is created, which results in a lack of empathy toward his employees.[1]

Undervaluing the worth of their employees coupled with poor empathy makes it painless for managers to enact their functional, bottom-line role. They can push harder and harder for their workers to produce quicker, more efficiently, and less expensively. *The result can*

lead to unrealistic expectations that in turn lead employees to take
short cuts, that is, act unethically.

Lynn Sharp Paine, professor of business administration at Harvard
Business School, writes how the managers of Sears, Roebuck & Company created unrealistic expectations for their employees in its Auto
Centers that led to blatant, ethical transgressions. In 1992, "attorneys
general in more than 40 states had accused the company of mislead-
ing customers and selling them unnecessary parts and services, from
brake jobs to front-end alignments."[2]

What happened? Due to diminishing profits and a market that had
become more competitive, management had given the service depart-
ments high, unrealistic sales quotas. If the workers failed to meet the
quotas, they could be transferred or have their hours reduced. These
unrealistic expectations, coupled with the threat of lower salary or
dislocation, pressured employees to push products that customers
didn't need.[3]

Power can cause executives to devalue their employees. When this
happens, the executive's reflexive role that necessitates making profit
may become unchecked; the executive pushes his or her employees
too hard and too fast. To cope with the pressure, employees may then
take unethical short cuts.

THROUGHOUT HISTORY, moral *justification* has been used to sanction acts of evil. Torture and murder have been committed for the sake of protecting one's family or honor, purifying the race, safeguarding a way of life, serving God, and so on. For example, in Rwanda in 1994, under the *justification* of "Hutu Power," approximately seventy thousand Tutsis were brutally killed.[1]

As mentioned in the section "Tyranny of Goals," B.F. Goodrich became embroiled in a scandal when it landed a contract with the U.S. government to provide brakes for fighter planes and pushed defective brakes through quality assurance to meet contract deadlines. Kermit Vandivier, who worked in the Goodrich test laboratory, testified against the company at a government hearing in 1969. He later wrote an expose of the scandal in *Harper's Magazine* in 1972. Vandivier's job description entailed issuing a "formal qualification report" following successful testing. The defective brakes had gone through testing on thirteen separate occasions—each time failing to pass government requirements. Halfway through the fourteenth attempt, it was obvious that the brakes would fail again. At this point, engineer Searle Lawson asked Vandivier to begin to prepare "engineering curves and graphic displays that were normally incorporated in a qualification report." Vandivier refused and went to his boss, Ralph Gretzinger, and told him about the situation. Gretzinger was furious and went to his boss. An hour passed and Gretzinger returned. Looking dejected, he said to Vandivier, "I've always believed that ethics and integrity were every bit as important as theorems and formulas, and never once has anything happened to change my beliefs. Now this . . . *Hell, I've got two sons I've got to put through school. . . .*" [Italics added.][2]

Notice how Gretzinger's *justification* is a *conflict of loyalty* (Trap 10). *Conflicts of loyalty* are often used as *justifications*. A common one in business is, "We have to do this to safeguard the company and the jobs of our employees" (to the detriment of shareholders).

After his *justification*, Gretzinger continued to talk to Vandivier. In a hoarse voice he said to him, "The way it stands now, we're to go ahead and prepare the data and other things for the graphic presentation in the report, and when we're finished, someone upstairs will actually write the report. After all . . . we're just drawing some curves, and what happens to them after they leave here—well, we're not responsible for that."[3] Do you recognize this trap? It's *indirect responsibility*, Trap 3.

In 1964 researchers Timothy Brock and Arnold Buss conducted an experiment that tested the influence of *justification*. Eighty subjects participated in the study. Subjects were run through the experiment one at a time. Upon arrival, participants met up with what they believed to be another subject (actually a confederate). Unbeknownst to the subjects, half of them had been preassigned to a "justification condition." Subjects in this condition began the experiment by taking a short test titled "California Aptitude Test for Supervisors, Trainers, and Teachers." Upon completing this test, regardless of their actual scores, subjects were told, "Your score shows that your aptitude for training and supervising others is very high, higher than 90 percent of others who have taken this test according to national norms. . . . Since the task today involves training another person, I am going to ask you to be the experimenter."[4]

The "experimenter" was to deliver shocks to the "student" (the confederate) when he responded incorrectly to a verbal test. The subject and confederate were separated visually by a screen. Ten levels of shock intensity were used and the confederate would loudly gasp each time the intensity level was six or greater. (Of course, no shock was actually delivered to the confederate.) Prior to commencing, the subject received the first five levels of shock to get a feeling for how painful they actually were.

At the end of the experiment, subjects filled out a series of questionnaires. Results indicated that subjects who had been given the *justification* that they were "superior supervisors" felt less guilt about the delivery of the "shocks" and estimated the "injury" to the confederate as significantly lower than the subjects who did not receive a justification.[5]

OBLIGATION is a particular type of *justification*. The diction-
ary definition of "obligation" is fulfilling a promise or commitment. Unethical behavior is readily given a moral connotation with
the use of *obligation*: "I needed to keep my commitment, to do what
I promised. My word is who I am."

In the Brock and Buss experiment described in the previous section, subjects were also preassigned to either a *high-shock condition*
or a *low-shock condition*. Those in the high-shock condition were told
to administer shock intensities of 6–10 to the "student" (confederate)
and those in the low-shock condition to use shock intensities of 1–5
when the "student" made errors.

Results from the questionnaires taken at the end of the experiment
demonstrated that those subjects in the high-shock condition felt much
more "obligated" to continue with the experiment compared to subjects in the low-shock condition.[1] Subjects used *obligation* as a *justification* for harming others. The more harm they inflicted, the more
"obligated" they felt.

Obligation can often be a *justification* that results from *obedience
to authority* (Trap 1). "My boss told me to do this and I said yes. I'm
obligated to follow through—I won't break my commitments."

PART II:
DEFENSIVE TRAPS

The seventeen traps described in Part II change our perception or give us ways to sidestep our guilt and shame, setting us up for repeated unethical behavior. Although some of these traps can cause us to behave unethically, they usually affect us *after* our wrongdoing.

ANNIHILATION OF GUILT

WE ALL SEE OURSELVES as above average morally. When we get caught in one of the traps described in Part I, we commit an immoral transgression. This causes us to feel guilt and shame. These feelings are painful. One way we reduce our negative feelings is by using Traps 25 through 37 in this section. There are also more fundamental ways that we annihilate guilt.

TRAP 21: ANGER

Researcher Martin Hoffman "argues that the roots of morality are to be found in empathy." The capacity for being able to feel what others are feeling, to see through the eyes of others, impels us to maintain high moral standards.[1] Hoffman defines empathy as "the involuntary, at times forceful, experiencing of another person's emotional state."[2] Hoffman defines guilt as an empathic response to someone's distress (feeling some of the same distress that the other feels) along with the awareness that one is the cause of the person's distress.[3] A lack of guilt, then, seems to be tied to a lack of empathy.

Hostility and excessive *anger* seem to squelch empathy and guilt. Paul Miller and Nancy Eisenberg from Arizona State University reviewed a large body of research and concluded in their summary that people high in empathy are low in hostility and vice versa: people who are hostile are low in empathy.[4]

In relationships, unless blatant abuse is going on, *anger* is most often a cover-up emotion. *Anger* is a secondary emotion that hides more vulnerable feelings. The vulnerable emotions are the motors for the *anger*. People get angry to protect themselves, to cover up their vulnerability. This process happens so quickly that people are usually unaware that their *anger* is obscuring other emotions.

Some of the most important, vulnerable emotions in relationships are *anxiety* (I'm going to lose you); *shame* (I blew it again, something's wrong with me); and *helplessness* (No matter what I do or say, I can't influence you). Robert Hoyk, coauthor of this book, is a psychologist who sees a fair share of couples in private practice. When Dr. Hoyk is working with couples, the trick is to find these vulnerable emotions underneath the *anger* and help the couple express them. In so doing, communication is reestablished. The vulnerable emotions are the tender feelings—the substance of empathic awareness. *Anger* is a powerful emotion and quickly obliterates these more tender emotions. *Anger* covers up or annihilates our more vulnerable emotions, thus destroying our capacity for empathy—which in turn annihilates our guilt.

Three years ago, the front page of *The New York Times* had an article by Kurt Eichenwald about the plea bargain of Richard Causey, former chief accounting officer at Enron. Causey had pleaded guilty to securities fraud and faced up to seven years in prison.

At a top-level Enron management meeting in September 2001, a red-faced Richard A. Causey, the chief accounting officer, pounded the table after hearing his colleagues label the company's accounting practices as "aggressive." According to executives in the room, Mr. Causey fumed that he considered such criticism a personal affront. . . .

Yesterday, more than four years later, Mr. Causey entered a Houston courtroom and pleaded guilty. . . . [5]

It's plausible that the *anger* Causey expressed in Enron's management meeting annihilated his deeper feelings of guilt and shame.

TRAP 22: GOING NUMB

In a therapy session, Susan was telling Dr. Hoyk how her father had beaten her as a child. Tears welled up in her eyes. Dr. Hoyk could see that her breathing was shallow. She covered her face with her hand as her head dropped forward. "I remember him grabbing me by the hair and throwing me against the wall!" She began to sob deeply. Suddenly she looked up and uncovered her face, eyes wide, and quickly looked down. The sobbing had abruptly stopped.

"What's happening Susan?" Dr. Hoyk asked gently.

"I don't know. I—it's gone. I don't feel a thing. I'm numb."

People who have experienced trauma often shut down painful feelings. How are they able to do this? Usually, it's something they've learned as children and it's become so automatic that they're not even aware they do it. Most often they make it happen by tensing the muscles in their upper bodies and shifting their mental attention quickly to something else.

Every emotion has an affiliated physical sensation. When we tense our muscles we kill our physical sensations. When we rapidly shift our mental attention, we extinguish the beliefs and thoughts associated with the emotion.

With time, Dr. Hoyk discovered that Susan would tighten the muscles in her solar plexus until they became "like a rock." She would often shift her thinking to something in the room or to thinking about plans for later in the day.

Early in his career as a psychologist, Dr. Hoyk worked on the "front lines," in several crisis centers and with the homeless population (he often called for police backup). Many times he treated people who had criminal records. These clients frequently had an uncanny ability to shut down their feelings. They had been in dangerous or unlawful situations that demanded they show no emotions.

It's not only "street people" or people who have suffered trauma that shut down their feelings. Many of us do this, especially if we were raised in families in which certain emotions weren't tolerated. If you were raised in a family that didn't express sadness, fear, or hurt—or worse, in a family that would actively discourage these emotions—it's likely that you've learned to shut down your feelings to some extent.

Tensing our muscles and shifting our mental focus, then, can be another way we annihilate our guilt.

TRAP 23: ALCOHOL

In research, when subjects have been asked to write an essay that supported an opinion that was completely opposite to their moral values—for example, an essay opposing more funding for handicapped facilities—and given the opportunity to drink *alcohol* after writing the essay, they usually would.[1]

Alcohol is an efficient way of extinguishing our feelings of guilt. The number one cause of relapse in alcoholics is negative emotions. One of the main reasons people become addicted to *alcohol* is to manage their bad feelings.

Although "power lunches" in the business world are a thing of the past, *alcohol* is still laced through the long hours and stress of the corporate environment. Bernie Ebbers, CEO of WorldCom, sentenced to twenty-five years in prison for an $11 billion accounting fraud, "was known to stay up drinking half the night with colleagues, even before board meetings."[2] It's possible that Ebbers deadened his feelings of guilt with *alcohol*.

TRAP 24: DESENSITIZATION

Bethany McLean and Peter Elkind, in their book *The Smartest Guys in the Room*, write about one of the tricks that Enron used with their accounting. In the following excerpt, Richard Causey, chief accounting officer, meets with an executive in an attempt to "delay recording losses."

At one meeting, an executive recalled, Causey kept coming back to a dead deal and asking: Was it possible the deal was still alive?

It wasn't, responded the executive.

"So there's no chance of it coming back?"

No.

"Is there even a *little* bit of a chance of it coming back?" asked Causey. "Do you want to look at it again?"

Finally the executive would take the hint—and the deal was declared undead. Enron deferred the hit for another quarter. "You did it once, it smelled bad," says the executive. "*You did it again, it didn't smell bad.*" [Italics added.][1]

Notice that the second time the executive resurrects a deal, it doesn't "smell bad." Over time, with repeated exposure, we emotionally habituate to any type of distress—including guilt.

If a psychotherapist is working with a client who has experienced trauma, one of the techniques he or she uses is to have the client retell the story over and over so the client becomes desensitized to the fear and anguish that is stimulated by the memory. You see a horror film once, it's scary. You see it six times, and it loses its punch. The same pattern is true for guilt. You commit a transgression once, it engenders guilt; you commit the transgression again and again, your guilt is deadened.

MINIMIZING makes unethical transgressions seem smaller. The person who minimizes admits that he or she did something wrong but states, "It's not that big of a deal." *Minimizing* is one of the most common ways we reduce our feelings of guilt and worthlessness resulting from transgressions.

TRAP 25: REDUCTION WORDS
In the winter of 2002, Martha Stewart, the CEO of a $250 million company, was indicted with obstruction of justice regarding insider trading. Stewart had sold her holdings of ImClone stock right before the value of the stock plummeted. Stewart had lied to investigators; she denied having received incriminating information from her broker's assistant, Douglas Faneuil. The day Stewart had sold her stock, Faneuil had called and told her that he had been on the phone all morning with the family of Sam Waksal, the former ImClone CEO. The Waksals were urgently trying to sell their ImClone stock prior to new regulations. Stewart was not charged with insider trading but was indicted for lying.[1]

Stewart's indictment hit major newspapers and magazines throughout the nation. She was quoted as saying that her sale of ImClone stock was *"a small personal matter."*[2]

In the preceding example, Stewart used the word *small*. Following is a list of words that we often use to minimize unethical behavior:

sort of
at most
barely
no big deal
not more than
only a little
merely
all I did was
kind of
once
just
maybe
hardly
I might have[3]

TRAP 26: RENAMING

Renaming is the use of benign or benevolent words to replace words that have negative connotations. A common *renaming* in the politics of war is the use of the phrase *collateral damage*. We all know that this phrase signifies death and physical injury to civilians, but using the words *collateral damage* removes us from the horror of its meaning. *Renaming* camouflages unethical transgressions. Sometimes *renaming* can even give a transgression a wholesome connotation.[1]

Audiotapes released by the Snohomish County Public Utility District in the State of Washington testify to the use of *renaming* by employees of Enron. In one transcript, two employees, Greg and Shari, are talking about preparations in relation to a future contract with Snohomish County.

Greg:[I]t's all how well you can weave these lies together, Shari.
Shari: I feel like I'm being corrupted now.
Greg: No, this is marketing.
Shari: O.K.[2]

Notice how Greg renames *lies* as *marketing*. This begins the process of changing his and Shari's perceptions about what they are doing. *Reduction words* and *renaming* influence our thinking and perceptions; they help maintain a positive view of ourselves.

TRAPS 27 AND 28: ADVANTAGEOUS COMPARISON AND ZOOMING OUT

Albert Bandura, one of the most respected researchers in psychology today, has conceptualized a strategy that he calls "advantageous comparison." *Advantageous comparison* allows the individual who has committed an unethical transgression to lessen his guilt by comparing what he has done to something worse. For example, "Damaging some property is no big deal when you consider that others are beating people up."[1]

The contrast doesn't necessarily have to be something worse—it can simply be a contrast with the big picture. We call this particular type of contrast *zooming out*.

Zooming out is like the function of a computer program that zooms out from a small, specific area of a map so that the view progressively encompasses more and more area—from a street intersection, to a view of a city, to a view of a county, to a view of several counties, and so on. Then the person contrasts the big picture with the street intersection and realizes how trivial the small area is in comparison to the larger view.

Michael Lewis in his book *Liar's Poker* writes about his days as a trader for Salomon Brothers in London. In Lewis's first few months after joining the firm, an experienced trader takes advantage of his naiveté and directs him to sell a large inventory of AT&T bonds to one of his new customers, a German investment banker. Unbeknownst to Lewis, the inventory belongs to the Salomon Brothers and is losing money. In the sale of the bonds, the losses are transferred to Lewis's client. When he realizes what has happened, Lewis uses *zooming out* to appease his guilt. He writes:

There was a convenient way of looking at this situation . . . Anyway, who was hurt besides my German? . . . The German's bank had lost sixty thousand dollars. The bank's shareholders, the Austrian Government, were therefore the losers. But compared with the assets of the nation as a whole, sixty thousand dollars was a ridiculously small sum.[2]

TRAP 29: "EVERYBODY DOES IT"

Thomas Gabor, professor of criminology at the University of Ottawa, interviewed employees who had illegally stolen equipment and materials from their jobs. A common rationalization was exemplified by the following employee's statement: "We are as good as management. They commit employee theft. Everybody does it. If I don't take it, someone else will."[1]

Psychologists call this type of rationalization the *False Consensus Effect*. When we do something that is unethical, we appease our guilt by falsely assuming that it's something everyone does. It's another way we minimize our transgressions—it's not that bad, it's something that happens all the time! The insidious thing about the False Consensus Effect (as with most other traps) is that we actually believe our own self-deception.

Gina Agostinelli, at the University of New Mexico, conducted an interesting experiment that validated the False Consensus Effect. Two hundred and thirty-five subjects were participants in her study. Subjects had been randomly assigned to either of two conditions: a *failure condition* or a *neutral condition*. Agostinelli administered to the subjects a test that was described as a "decision-making problem that many career centers use to help companies hire employees . . . a valid indicator of future job success that measured general problem-solving abilities under time pressure." Following the test, subjects in the failure condition were given false feedback: your "score is poor and indicates that you are not good at solving problems under time pressure and cannot make important decisions efficiently." Subjects in the neutral condition were given no feedback.

All subjects were then given a questionnaire that asked them to estimate how well the general public would do on the problem-solving test.

The magnitude of the False Consensus Effect was impressive. In the neutral condition, 40 percent of subjects estimated that the public would be successful with the problem-solving test. In the failure condition, subjects estimated that only 15 percent of the public would be successful! Subjects who "failed" the test estimated that a large number of people would also fail the test. "If I fail, most people would."[2]

TRAP 30: "WE WON'T GET CAUGHT"

When the risk of getting caught for an ethical or legal transgression is low, our perception of wrongdoing is often minimized. Joseph Badaracco, professor of ethics at Harvard Business School, in his book *Business Ethics* presents the case study of Don Taylor, a new employee of the International Drilling Corporation (IDC) who witnessed the use of this type of minimization.

In October of 1971, Taylor was present at a meeting with the president of the company, Jeff Williams, and a vice president, Brian Rosenberg. Rosenberg informed Williams of specific actions by the company which had happened in the previous year that violated the securities laws. Rosenberg told Williams not to worry—the company's "tracks were covered." Taylor's superiors advocated that they do nothing because their chances of being caught were low.[1]

When we were children, most of our moral decisions were made based on our desire to avoid punishment and to gain rewards. As adults, we're more apt to base our moral decisions on other factors. But after we've committed a transgression, our early conditioning is an undercurrent that influences our perception. When the chance of being punished is low, the sting of unethical behavior seems less serious and we tend to minimize the importance of the transgression.

TRAP 31: "WE DIDN'T HURT THEM THAT BAD"

A particular type of minimization is *minimizing* the harm done by one's unethical behavior.

Timothy Brock and Arnold Buss's experiment, which we described in the section on *justification*, explored this type of minimization. To review, subjects were run through the experiment one at a time. Upon arrival, a participant met up with what he or she thought was another subject (actually a confederate). The real subject was given the role of the *experimenter* and the confederate played the *student* role.

The subject was to deliver shocks to the "student" when that person responded incorrectly to a verbal test. There were ten levels of shock intensity. Unbeknownst to the subjects, half of them had been preassigned to a *high-shock condition* and the other half to a *low-shock condition*. Those in the high-shock condition were told to use shock intensities of 6 to 10 and those in the low-shock condition to use shock intensities of 1 to 5.

Results from questionnaires taken at the end of the experiment demonstrated that those subjects in the high-shock condition estimated that "injury" to the student was significantly less compared to estimates of harm from subjects in the low-shock condition![1]

The higher the shock intensities used, the more apt the subject was inclined to minimize the harmful consequences. The more injury our unethical behavior causes, the more we're likely to minimize our perception of harm done.

Remember the example in "Advantageous Comparison and Zooming Out"? Trader Michael Lewis used the technique of *zooming out* to minimize his guilt. The focus of his *minimizing* was the amount of harm incurred. When referring to the "Austrian Government" as the loser, he writes, "But compared with the assets of the nation as a whole, sixty thousand dollars was a ridiculously small sum." In other words, *"we didn't hurt them that bad."*

TRAP 32: SELF-SERVING BIAS
The *self-serving bias* is what causes us to say "Yes, what happened was wrong, but it wasn't my fault." It's our tendency to take credit for success and to attribute failure to external causes. When we externalize blame—more often than not—it's not a lie, it's something we actually believe.

We all have the tendency to blame others when we fail or do wrong. Seventy scientific studies involving 6,949 subjects have verified the *self-serving bias*.[1] When we blame others for our transgressions, we maintain a positive view of ourselves—we annihilate our guilt. Sometimes the person we blame is responsible for some of the wrongdoing, but we shift *all* the blame onto them to uphold our innocence. In some instances, "victims get blamed for bringing suffering on themselves."[2]

We all see ourselves as above average morally. When we act unethically, our behavior becomes a threat to the positive view we have of ourselves. Besides feelings of guilt and worthlessness, one of the predominant emotions that we experience from this threat to our integrity is feeling irritated all the time.[3] Irritation (that is, *anger*) is an emotion that automatically shifts our attention externally. The threat is no longer within but without—we quickly latch onto outside causes for our distress.

In August of 2000, 6.5 million Firestone tires on Ford Explorers were recalled in response to allegations that the tires caused fatal accidents. Following the recall, the Ford Motor Company began an analysis of approximately 13 million Firestone tires that were still being utilized on Ford Explorers and trucks.

In May of 2001, Ford met with Firestone to talk "about tire safety." Firestone didn't want to talk about tire safety but wanted to talk about the Ford Explorer: "We told them our concerns, asked them again to please look at the vehicle. They said no."

After publicly blaming each other, Firestone ended its business relationship with Ford—a relationship that had been ongoing for ninety-five years. Ford announced that it "did not have confidence in the tire" and replaced the thirteen million tires still in use.[4]

Minimization is the most common defensive trap. When we act unethically, we trivialize the wrongdoing. One way we do this is by putting the blame on someone or something else just like Firestone did about their tires.

Sometimes we blame the situation instead of others. As we've already seen, many of the Primary Traps are situational in nature. Therefore, ironically, the situation may actually be the true culprit. For example, "I was running so fast because there was so much pressure to meet my deadline. I wasn't even aware that an ethical dilemma existed!" (Trap 15) Even though this assertion may be correct, blaming circumstances can be another manifestation of the *self-serving bias*, one more way we try and minimize transgressions in an effort to reduce our guilt and shame.

TRAP 33:

ADDICTION

I N 1 9 6 1 the Federal District Court in Philadelphia sent seven top executives from the electrical industry to prison for price-fixing. It was the largest antitrust case in the history of the United States. Attorney General Robert Kennedy publicly stated, "I regard the price-fixing of the electrical industry as a major serious threat to democracy." Led by General Electric and Westinghouse, the conspiracy involved twenty-nine corporations. Author John Fuller, in his book *The Gentlemen Conspirators*, writes:

Forty-five executives of some of the country's outstanding corporations got together over a long period of years in conspiratorial meetings. They set the meetings up from public phone booths, or by letters on blank stationery signed by coded names. They never permitted themselves to be seen together in public dining rooms or hotel lobbies. They often registered in hotels as individuals, rather than as company representatives. . . . The conspirators were required to destroy immediately any written communications . . . to cover up their tracks with falsified expense accounts. . . . The extent of the criminal practices was so widespread in the industry that they affected nearly every generator, every electrical distributor, every utility, power plant, dam, power-line pole, and power transformer, and thus every home and industry in the country.[1]

In an interview, one of the key people in the conspiracy, a General Electric vice president, stated that he knew the price-fixing was wrong, but while he was involved, he kept telling himself that he was "going to quit" after profits "stabilized." He'd say to himself, "I'll start next week on educating the boys, on warning them of the dangers of keeping this up. I'll slowly guide them out of this, so that we can forget it ever happened." Needless to say, he never did stop. Like a heroin addict, he kept telling himself, *"I'll stop tomorrow."*

Why do people become addicted? Dr. Hoyk, the primary author of this book, treats addiction problems in his private practice. He always asks addicts, "What do you like about the drug? What does it do for you? How does it help you?" Most people become addicted to a substance or an activity because of short-term benefits. The activity or drug often solves a problem in the short term, even if it makes the problem worse in the long term.

At the beginning of his career, Dr. Hoyk was employed in an outpatient clinic for drug addiction in which he led a weekly group. One of his clients, Jim, would rarely say anything. Jim was a bright, handsome man who had a good job in a hospital. One evening at the end of the group meeting, he came up to Dr. Hoyk when everyone had left and told him his story. He said, "Dr. Hoyk, I have a hard time speaking up in the group." As he spoke his voice wavered. "I get very anxious speaking in front of others—I'm really shy. I'm anxious even speaking to you now. But you know, when I shoot up, I love myself. I'm so confident. When I'm high, I can sit down on a public bench and lead a conversation with a total stranger for an hour—I love who I am." Jim's problem of chronic shyness disappeared when he used drugs. The dramatic, short-term benefits of the drug kept him coming back for more.

The benefits the GE executive received—status, security, a large salary, a profitable company—also kept him addicted to price-fixing. The executive stated that he faced vicious demands to keep annual profits up, and if he failed to do so, there was no doubt in his mind that he'd lose his job.

It's often painful to make decisions for the long term. A vice president of GE, George Burens, resisted the price-fixing. He was transferred, and his "salary was cut from $127,000 in 1958 to $40,000 in 1960." Later, Burens was forced to resign.

Burens was able to make difficult—but healthy—long-term decisions. Though tempted, he didn't allow himself to become addicted to immoral behavior. When he said to himself, *"I'll stop tomorrow,"* he did.

IF OUR FELLOW COWORKERS ignore, justify, or condone our unethical behavior, it supports our view that we didn't do anything wrong or that if we did, it's not that big a deal.

Ervin Staub, psychology professor at the University of Massachusetts, has written about the origins and prevention of genocide: "Research on individual behavior in emergencies . . . as well as the behavior of bystanders in actual life situations, like the rescuers of Jews in Nazi Europe . . . has demonstrated the great power and potential of bystanders to influence the behavior of other bystanders, and even of perpetrators."[1]

An experiment by Donna Gelfand at the University of Utah demonstrated how often we let transgressions slide. Subjects (180 men and 156 women) were adult shoppers in two drugstores in Salt Lake City. A shoplifter, a twenty-one-year-old confederate, gained the attention of an unsuspecting shopper by dropping a store item. The confederate was given a signal (from a hidden observer via a concealed radio communication) when the shopper was looking at her. She then stole several items, placing them in her handbag, and left the store in a hurry without stopping at the cash register. Shoppers were later questioned about the incident. All of the subjects had seen the shoplifting but *only 28 percent* of them had reported it![2]

If 72 percent of people don't report an illegal behavior by a total stranger, imagine the percentage of people who ignore transgressions in a business environment in which people work together as a team, especially if the transgressor is your boss, who has the power to fire you—whistleblowing can be "career suicide."[3]

L EE ROSS at Stanford University discovered that our *established impressions* of others (and it doesn't take a lot to establish these impressions) tend to endure even if we are convinced later that our impressions are wrong.

In Ross's experiment, subjects who took on the role of a "student" were given a verbal test one at a time and then given fake results as to how well they scored. At the end of the test, a third of the subjects were told that they had scored exceptionally well compared to the average person ("success condition"); another third were told that they scored way below the average ("failure condition"); and the final third were told that they scored equal to the average person ("average condition"). *At the end of the experiment, the researcher then told the subjects that the results were bogus—that is, that they had been given fake test scores.*

Unbeknownst to each "student" taking the test, there was another subject who was observing the experiment through a one-way mirror. The observer's task was to document the student's answers and speed of response, and rate the student's confidence in answering the test questions. Of course, the observer heard the initial scores of the student and later, at the end of the study, heard the experimenter tell the student that the feedback was false.

After dismissing the student, the researcher joined up with the observer and gave a pencil-and-paper questionnaire to the observer to fill out. The questionnaire asked the observer to estimate the student's actual score on the test, the score of an average person, and how well the student would have scored on another, similar test.

Results indicated that observers rated the students in accordance to their initial impressions that had been established before the students were told that they had received false feedback. In other words, even after the observers knew that the results of the students' tests were bogus, they rated the students in the success condition as being more capable and rated the students in the failure condition as being much less capable![1] Our *established impressions* often stick even in the face of contradictory evidence.

ROBERT HARE, one of the foremost experts in the area of *psychopathy*, gives an example in his book *Without a Conscience* of a psychopath in the business world. The example was made available by Paul Babiak, an industrial psychologist in New York.

Dave is described as an employee who was originally liked by his immediate coworkers in his department, but after working with him for two years, his colleagues mistrusted him. He frequently displayed "disruptive," angry "outbursts," was "self-centered, unreliable," "irresponsible," and "manipulative." Some of his coworkers stated that "virtually everything he said was a lie and his promises were never to be believed."

When Babiak interviewed Dave, he talked about "himself as a hard worker, a strong leader, a 'team builder,' honest, intelligent, the guy responsible for really 'making' the department."

Dave's direct supervisor was exasperated by his behavior. The supervisor arranged a test of honesty with an executive of the company. The two of them decided that Dave's supervisor should relay specific information to Dave and then the executive should meet with Dave individually. When the executive met with Dave and asked him how the meeting went with his supervisor, Dave replied with information that was completely "distorted." The executive was persuaded that Dave was indeed dishonest.

But reprisal for Dave's behavior was thwarted by top executives; "those higher up in the organization had been convinced—by Dave— of his management talent and potential. Despite clear evidence of dishonesty, they were still 'charmed' by him."[2]

Even though coworkers in Dave's department over time had learned to mistrust him due to his blatant, repetitive dishonesty, the favorable, *established impressions* of upper management endured in the face of contradictory evidence.

CONTEMPT FOR THE VICTIM

THROUGHOUT THE HISTORY of humanity, religious, gender, and racial minorities have often been regarded as subhuman by those in power. They have been labeled as "gooks," "savages," "cockroaches," and worse. When we dehumanize others we lose our empathy toward them and see them as objects without hopes or feelings.[1] When we lose our empathy for others it is easier to harm them without feeling guilt.

An ingenious experiment was conducted by Albert Bandura at Stanford University in 1975. (This study is the same experiment as the one cited in the section "Lost in the Group." Here we're emphasizing results not written about in this earlier section.) Each time the experiment was run, a group of three subjects played the role of "supervisors." The task of the subject-supervisors was to "punish" a small group of decision makers—located in an adjacent room—by shocking them when they made poor decisions. (The decision makers didn't really exist.)

After explaining the purpose of the experiment, the researcher left the subject-supervisors, telling them he was going to the adjacent room where the decision makers were and that he would further communicate via intercom. Later the subject-supervisors heard the experimenter over the intercom make a descriptive comment about the decision makers to his lab assistant after "accidentally" leaving his microphone on.

Subjects ("supervisors") had been randomly divided into three different conditions. A third of the subjects heard at this point the experimenter commenting that the decision makers seemed like "an animalistic, rotten bunch" ("dehumanized condition"). Another third of the subjects heard the experimenter comment that the decision makers seemed like a "perceptive" and "understanding" group ("humanized condition"). And the last third of the subjects heard no comment from the researcher ("neutral condition").

Results indicated that the subjects in the "dehumanized condition" shocked the decision makers with the greatest intensity! Subjects in the "neutral condition" shocked the decision makers with less intensity and in the "humanized condition" subjects used very little intensity![2]

Michael Lewis in his book *Liar's Poker* writes vividly about his days as a trader for Salomon Brothers in London. In the culture of trading, customers were referred to as "victims," "fools," "stupid," or "ducks . . . that were trained to fly repeatedly over the same field of hunters until shot dead." Traders were trained "to exploit the weakness in others." "If people were scared or desperate, he [the trader] herded them like sheep into a corner, then made them pay for their uncertainty."

Lewis described a cultural "policy of screwing investors." If the company held a position (for example a large inventory of AT&T bonds) that was losing money, the company would, at times, sell the position to a trusting customer, thereby transferring the losses to the customer.[3] The culture of *dehumanizing customers* made this "policy" easier to do with less guilt, thus reinforcing a practice of unethical behavior.

Dehumanizing others seems to be cyclical. In other experiments, after subjects administered electric shocks to a victim (once again to a confederate who acted as if he was being shocked), the subjects later had a tendency to degrade him. Subjects knew the victim had done nothing wrong but needed to persuade themselves that he somehow deserved the punishment—thus, they derogated him.[4] In the experiment that was described in Trap 1, "Obedience to Authority," the researcher Stanley Milgram writes:

Many subjects harshly devalued the victim *as a consequence* of acting against him. Such comments as, "He was so stupid and stubborn he deserved to get shocked," were common. Once having acted against the victim, these subjects found it necessary to view him as an unworthy individual, whose punishment was made inevitable by his own deficiencies of intellect and character.[5]

So the more we dehumanize others, the easier it is to harm them, and the more we harm them, the more we dehumanize them.

REMEMBER TRAP 17, "Enacting a Role"? Students put on the role of prison guards and after six days in a realistic prison setting began to "disparage" the prisoners (other students) and devise "cruel and degrading routines." Often what we do is what we become. Frequently, we observe our own behavior (what we do or say). In so doing, we influence our attitudes (negative or positive feelings about our action). Social psychologist David Myers writes, "Hearing myself talk informs me of my attitudes; seeing my actions provides clues to how strong my beliefs are."[1]

When coauthor Dr. Hoyk was in graduate school, his professor of social psychology, Dr. Dalenberg, told his class that early in her career, she had considered walking up and down the aisles of the classroom during exams to catch students cheating. She ultimately decided not to do this. Why? She knew that after a while, her behavior would shape her attitudes—she would probably become—to some degree—more suspicious of her students.

Eric Storch at Columbia University administered a questionnaire to 244 students. Answering the questionnaire anonymously, the college students were asked how often they had copied other student's work, plagiarized, and cheated on exams. The questionnaire also asked the students to rate their approval on a scale of 1 to 5 ("strongly disapprove" to "strongly approve") of these three transgressions.

Results indicated that students who reported more academic dishonesty gave significantly higher approval ratings of their dishonesty![2] When we act unethically, we automatically begin to view our transgressions in a less negative way.

In 2001, Enron deceived California customers during the energy crisis. The federal government had ordered power plants to maintain full output capacity. Enron created false electrical shortages by shutting down plants and in so doing ran up prices. The company made billions of dollars from the illegal scam. The main players in the scam were the West Coast energy traders who bought and sold electricity and scheduled its delivery. "The attitude was, 'play by your own rules,' says a former trader. We all did it. We talked about it openly . . . We took *pride* in getting around the rules." [Italics added.] Notice in this example that unethical behavior became so frequent that traders were proud of their actions. It's possible that one of the reasons why they "took pride in getting around the rules" is that they became trapped in *doing is believing.*[3]

Doing is believing doesn't happen if we're ordered to do something. It only works when we feel like we have freely chosen to act. If your boss orders you to lie and you obey, your attitudes about your lying won't change. You'll say to yourself, "Lying isn't something I usually do. I did it because my boss pressured me to do it."

If we choose to act unethically, the act itself will shape our beliefs and attitudes about our transgression. It's possible—to some degree—that we will begin to see the transgression as more acceptable.

PART III:
PERSONALITY TRAPS

The following part describes various personality traits that can make us more vulnerable to wrongdoing. Most of these traits interact with situational pressure. Without situational influence, their impact on our behavior is usually minimal.

TRAP 38:

PSYCHOPATHY

A RE THE LEADERS in corporate scandals psychopaths? Do these leaders have criminal personalities? Are they born with defects that predispose them to breaking the law? What is a psychopath?

When we think of a psychopath, it conjures up images of "Hannibal the Cannibal" played by Anthony Hopkins in *The Silence of the Lambs*. Hannibal is a disturbing serial killer, with an emotionless, twisted mind. Such portrayals of psychopaths have their counterparts in reality: Jeffrey Dahmer, who tortured, murdered, and maimed fifteen boys and men; Ted Bundy, who confessed to murdering thirty women; or John Gacy, voted as "Man of the Year" by his local Chamber of Commerce, who killed thirty-two men and buried most of them underneath his house.[1]

Serial killers are very uncommon. Robert Hare, who developed the Psychopathy Checklist, an instrument used by psychologists to diagnose psychopaths, estimates that there are less than a hundred serial killers in the United States and Canada combined. He estimates that there are up to three million psychopaths in the United States and Canada that are more the "garden-variety type."[2]

THE GARDEN-VARIETY PSYCHOPATH is diagnosed by psychologists and psychiatrists as having an *Antisocial Personality Disorder*.

There are very specific criteria that need to be met for someone to be labeled with this disorder:

Since the age of 15, persistent "violation of the rights of others" as exemplified by at least three of the following:

    1. [Acts of unlawful behavior]

    2. [Frequent deceit]

    3. Impulsivity.

    4. Aggressiveness.

    5. Reckless disregard for safety.

    6. Consistent irresponsibility.

    7. Lack of remorse.[3]

Given that at least three of these criteria need to be present from the age of fifteen, it's highly unlikely that the leaders in these corporate scandals are psychopaths.

An important distinction needs to be made between those who have an Antisocial Personality Disorder and those who display antisocial behavior, that is, one of the seven symptoms just listed. Although occurrence of Antisocial Personality Disorder is about 4 percent in the population, the prevalence of people who display antisocial behavior in the population ranges from 5 to 15 percent.[4] Is antisocial *behavior* influenced by genetic factors? Are people born with certain traits that increase their risk of having a criminal record? The answer seems to be yes. This doesn't mean that the leaders who engineered business scandals have these genetic factors; it just means that genetics can influence the likelihood of criminal behavior.

Scientists are able to determine the heritability of human traits by studying the similarities of identical twins versus fraternal twins. Identical twins have identical genetics. For example, their eyes are all the same color. Approximately half of the DNA in fraternal twins is identical. This leads to the conclusion that traits which are highly similar in identical twins, but are not very similar in fraternal twins, are traits which are much more likely to be inherited.

Twins in these studies (both identical and fraternal) have been separated in their first year of life by adoption. Because they are reared in different environments, trait similarities are not attributable to environmental influences.[5]

So what have researchers found? If an adopted child's biological father has no criminal record nor does the adoptive father, the chance of the child growing up and having a criminal record is 10.5 percent.[6] This 10 percent is due to the traps in this book. If the child's adoptive father has a criminal record, but the biological father doesn't, then the chance that the child will become a criminal is only 11.5 percent. Being raised by a criminal father increases the child's potential of criminal behavior a negligible amount. But if the adopted child's biological father has a criminal record and the adoptive father doesn't, the chances are 22 percent that the child will become a criminal. In other words, *if you have genes from a criminal father, there's an 11 percent greater chance that you will have a criminal record as an adult.* (Note: If you have criminal genes and are raised by a father who has a criminal record, there's a 36 percent chance of becoming a criminal. Once you have criminal genes, there seems to be an additive effect in regard to parenting.)[7]

What are the genetic traits that increase our chance of committing crime? We don't know for sure. Sixty-seven percent of those who commit crimes have impulsive behavior. Lack of self-control seems to be a trait that is highly genetic. PET scans have demonstrated that brains of nonpsychopaths (when contrasted to brains of psychopaths) reveal greater activity "in areas responsible for impulse control."[8]

Fifty-eight percent of those who commit crimes display belligerent, hostile behavior. Hostility also is a trait that is very heritable.[9] Hostility and impulse control are interrelated. Without good impulse control, one is liable to be more hostile. Remember the description of Dave, the psychopath who was ultimately supported by upper management (see "Established Impressions")? Dave was someone who frequently displayed "disruptive" angry "outbursts."

TRAPS 39 AND 40:
POVERTY AND NEGLECT

A RNOLD ROGOW AND HAROLD LASSWELL, in their book
Power, Corruption, and Rectitude, reported on an analysis they
conducted of thirty political bosses "who dominated local governments
in the late nineteenth and early twentieth centuries." All of these bosses
had a history of corruption and scandal. The authors discovered two
main types of bosses. One type they called the "Game Politician" and
the other type they called the "Gain Politician."

The "Game Politician" had been raised in an emotionally neglect-
ful environment. In the family, there was little expression of love and
affection. Often the father was punitive and strict. Thinking back on
his childhood, the "Game Politician" could not remember times of
happiness. As an adult, the "Game Politician" was manipulative and
corrupt in politics so as to acquire "power, prestige, adulation, and a
sense of importance."

The "Gain Politician" had been raised in a family that was emotionally close but suffered from extreme poverty. In adulthood, the
"Gain Politician" was corrupt for personal, monetary gain.[1]

This analysis by Rogow and Lasswell is interesting, but it should
be regarded with caution. The investigation is not scientifically systematic. One cannot make any claims that neglect or poverty in childhood
causes corruption in adulthood. Nevertheless, the authors' premise
begs for further research that might indeed establish this fact.

It is interesting to note that Bernie Ebbers—CEO of WorldCom who was imprisoned for corporate fraud—came from a very poor upbringing, as did Ken Lay, the CEO of Enron. In Part IV of this book, we'll analyze the types of traps that were present in the shocking Jonestown mass suicide that took place in 1978. Reverend Jim Jones, who was the leader of Jonestown, experienced bitter, emotional neglect as a child.

TRAP 41:
LOW SELF-ESTEEM

WHEREAS inflated self-esteem can potentially lead to unethical behavior (see Trap 14, "Self-Enhancement") *low self-esteem* can also be a factor that can drive us to take unethical short cuts. Self-esteem is defined as "our overall self-evaluation."[1] People who tend to feel worthless are tempted to cheat or lie to boost the impressions they make on others in an attempt to feel better about themselves.

Researchers Deborah Kashy and Bella DePaulo had seventy community members anonymously keep track of the number of lies they told during a week-long period by keeping a diary. Subjects told between zero and forty-six lies, averaging one lie per day; 25 percent of these were "white lies"—lies that are told to enhance a friend's self-esteem. Participants completed ten different personality measures. It was found that subjects lied mostly to create a good impression of themselves socially.[2]

An intriguing experiment was conducted by Elliot Aronson and David Mettee at the University of Texas in 1968. These researchers manipulated subjects' temporary self-esteem by giving them false, negative feedback on a personality test. Subjects were then given an opportunity to cheat at a card game that would allow them to win money. Those who had received feedback that deflated their self-esteem were more apt to cheat.[3]

S OMETIMES leaders can have personalities that are *authoritarian*. This trait can actually be measured by a questionnaire that psychologist Bob Altemeyer has created—the RWA-Scale. These leaders often grew up in a family that emphasized "dominance and *obedience to authority*." [Italics added.] As children, authoritarian leaders were taught to be "respectful" and "dutiful," and if they disobeyed, they would often receive severe punishment. An example of one of the questions on the RWA-Scale is, "Obedience and respect for authority are the most important virtues children should learn." Authoritarian leaders tend to be "aggressive or punitive" in their style.[1] They tend to adhere strongly to "traditional social norms."[2]

Executives who have authoritarian traits dominate groups, are highly directive, and tend to squelch any dissent. They have a difficult time tolerating opposition, disagreement, or resistance to their ideas and direction. When dissent is stifled, the influence of *conformity* (Trap 11) is magnified. Remember, in regard to *conformity*, if just one person voices disagreement with the group opinion, the influence of *conformity* drops by a factor of 28 percent! The authoritarian leader, then, fortifies the trap of *conformity* by squashing any dissent within the group.

TRAP 43:
SOCIAL DOMINANCE ORIENTATION

SOCIAL DOMINANCE ORIENTATION (SDO) is a trait that delineates one's "preference for inequality among social groups." It is the wish that the groups and organizations you belong to (business teams, corporation, social class, gender, ethnicity, country, and so on) be "superior" and "dominate." Unlike *authoritarianism*, which is "a desire for individual dominance," "SDO is regarded as the desire that some categories of people dominate others."[1] *Authoritarianism* is a trait that is interpersonal. People who are high in SDO aren't necessarily *authoritarian*. They can strive for equality when relating to people within their in-groups. But their perceptions of those outside their in-groups are significantly affected by this trait.

SDO can be measured by a questionnaire that has been developed by Felicia Pratto and her colleagues at Stanford University. People taking the questionnaire rate their positive or negative feelings on a scale of 1 to 7 (1 = "very negative"; 7 = "very positive") in reaction to sixteen statements. People who are high in SDO have a positive reaction to statements in the questionnaire such as "Some groups of people are simply inferior to other groups," "To get ahead in life, it is sometimes necessary to step on other groups," or "Inferior groups should stay in their place."

People who are high in SDO have poor empathy, tend to be intolerant of others, and are low in altruism. Pratto writes, "[O]ur data suggest that empathy with other persons may be a significant attenuator of SDO." Because altruism and empathy are often the royal roads to ethical behavior, people high in SDO are more apt to be unethical. SDO orients people in their political and social attitudes. People high in SDO, for example, are consistently against social programs, the rights of minorities, and environmental protection.[2]

TRAP 44:
NEED FOR CLOSURE

THE NEED FOR CLOSURE is "the desire for a definite answer on some topic, *any* answer as opposed to confusion and ambiguity."[1] It's the tendency to jump on the first opinion that comes to mind instead of tolerating a state of not knowing and taking the time to look at a problem or judgment from many different angles.

The *need for closure* is augmented under work conditions that make processing of information more difficult: *time pressure* (Trap 15), fatigue, and excessive background noise. When such conditions exist, it's more difficult to tolerate a state of confusion and ambiguity.

Although *need for closure* is influenced by situational factors, it is also a *personality* trait. Some people are more able to tolerate states of ambiguity than others. Arie Kruglanski has developed the Need for Closure Scale, which measures this *personality* dimension. Those high in the trait of *need for closure* are more apt to endorse items on the scale such as, "I usually make important decisions quickly and confidently," "I do not usually consult many different opinions before forming my own view," "When I'm confused about an important issue, I feel very upset," or "It's annoying to listen to someone who cannot seem to make up his or her mind."[2]

The *need for closure* magnifies the influence of Trap 34, "Coworker Reactions."

As previously stated, the trap *coworker reactions* is the tendency for our fellow coworkers to ignore, justify, or condone our unethical behavior. This tendency is influenced by *established impressions*.

As we also talked about before, *established impressions* of others tend to endure even if we are convinced later on that our impressions are wrong. So if we have positive feelings about our boss and later discover that he has done something unethical or illegal, we tend to stay with our first impressions and continue to view him in favorable terms. Our *established impressions* often stick, even in the face of contradictory evidence.

Established impressions are similar to biases in that they influence us by being readily available and accessible in our conscious thinking—they tend to jump into our minds and offer an answer with little effort.

Kruglanski and his colleagues have established that those who are high in the *need for closure* are more prone to stay with *established impressions* in the face of contradictory evidence.[3]

IN GENERAL this last trait, *empathy*, actually enhances our capacity for moral behavior. But sometimes we can get into trouble
when our empathic response overpowers our sense of fairness. But
before we look at this exception, let's take a look at the origins of this
important attribute.

Have you ever wondered why you respond reflexively to other
peoples' pain and difficulties? For example, your wife opens a jar of
leftovers that she's taken from the fridge. She smells the vegetables
and then quickly pulls her head away—her nose wrinkles with disgust. All of a sudden, you notice that you feel a bit nauseous. On another occasion, you're watching your son's baseball team play their
last game of the season. The pitcher throws a wild pitch, and the ball
hits the batter in the left shoulder. You automatically flinch and tense
your left arm.

In the 1990s a group of researchers from Italy discovered *mirror
neurons*. Conducting experiments with monkeys, these researchers
identified "a type of brain cell that responds equally when we perform
an action and when we witness someone else perform the same action." Because we can't easily implant electrodes in the human brain,
scientists aren't sure that mirror neurons exist in people. But we do
know "that humans have a more general mirror system."[1]

Researchers speculate that mirror neurons are the biological base of *empathy*. When you see your wife's nose wrinkle in disgust, perhaps there are mirror neurons firing in your brain that trigger a similar emotional state—your stomach begins to feel queasy.

Some people are more empathic than others. Mark Davis has developed a multidimensional *empathy* scale. The subscale "Empathic Concern" seems to be the most accurate in measuring trait differences in *empathy*. People high in *empathy* endorse items on the subscale such as, "I often have tender, concerned feelings for people less fortunate than me."[2]

DANIEL BATSON and his colleagues at the University of Kansas conducted an experiment that demonstrated that—at times—*empathy* can be a liability. Sixty subjects were asked to listen to an audiotape of Sheri, a "10-year-old" who had a fatal, "muscle-paralyzing disease." It was explained to subjects that the audiotape might be used in a radio broadcast by the Quality of Life Foundation, a "national organization devoted to helping improve the quality of life of children with terminal illnesses." The students were to evaluate the tape using an "emotional-reaction questionnaire." Results of the evaluation would help the Quality of Life Foundation decide if it would be an effective tape for radio.

Unbeknownst to the subjects, half of them had been assigned to a "high-empathy condition" and the other half to a "low-empathy condition." Those in the high-empathy condition were asked to listen to the tape and "try to imagine how the child who is interviewed feels about what has happened and how it has affected this child's life." Past research has demonstrated that this manipulation is successful in inducing *empathy*. Subjects in the low-empathy condition were asked to listen and "try to take an objective perspective toward what is described."

After the subjects had evaluated the tape, they were informed that the Quality of Life Foundation would be willing to give Sheri a better chance of receiving treatment. Subjects were told that the Quality of Life Foundation could only accept a limited number of children because of funding. The waiting list to be accepted was long; many of the children on the waiting list would die before being helped. Subjects were also informed that Sheri was at the bottom of the waiting list. As a favor for helping them evaluate the tape, the Quality of Life Foundation would be willing to move Sheri to the top of the list if subjects so desired.

Results indicated that subjects in the high-empathy condition were more likely to help Sheri "at the expense of others"! So under certain conditions, *empathy* can overpower our sense of justice and fairness. Justice is a crucial standard that guides our morality.

Following the experiment, after debriefing, subjects often told the researchers experiences from their own lives that were similar to the experimental dilemma. One subject described an incident at his employment "in which a supervisor's special feelings for one among a number of workers led to unfair partiality."[3] We probably can all think of times when we have seen someone promoted because they were the boss's friend.

PART IV:
ANALYZING DILEMMAS

In this last section of the book, we describe two dilemmas—
real-life stories of unethical behavior—and analyze them using
the traps in this book. The first dilemma, known as "The
Parable of the Sadhu," has been used in many business schools
to challenge the thinking of "tens of thousands of students."

The second story is Jonestown. In 1978, under
the leadership of Reverend Jim Jones, over nine
hundred people committed mass suicide.

Although these two examples are not from the business
world, their complexity provides an opportunity
to explicate the maximum number of traps.

THE PARABLE OF THE SADHU

THE FOLLOWING STORY was taken from a chapter written
by Bowen McCoy in the *Harvard Business Review on Corporate Ethics*.[1]

In 1982, Bowen McCoy, an investment banker for Morgan Stanley,
spent his sabbatical trekking in the Himalayan Mountains of Nepal
with a group of people from Japan, New Zealand, and Switzerland.
After hiking for thirty days, McCoy and his group reached a base
camp where they prepared to climb to the highest point of their trip,
"an 18,000 foot pass."

The next morning, the group started their assent at 3:30 A.M. to
conquer the most treacherous part of the pass *"before the sun melted
the steps cut in the ice."* [Italics added.] McCoy writes, "The Himalayas
were having their wettest spring in 20 years; hip-deep powder and ice
had already driven us off one ridge. If we failed to cross the pass, *I feared
that the last half of our once-in-a-lifetime trip would be ruined. . . .* I
felt strong—*my adrenaline was flowing. . . . if the ice steps had given
way, I would have slid down about 3,000 feet. . . ."* [Italics added.]

As the sun rose over the mountains, the group rested at 15,500 feet.
"One of the New Zealanders, who had gone ahead, came staggering
down toward us with a body slung across his shoulders. He dumped
the almost naked, barefoot body of an Indian holy man—a sadhu—
at my feet. He had found the pilgrim lying on the ice, shivering and

suffering from hypothermia. . . . *The New Zealander was angry. He wanted to get across the pass before the bright sun melted the snow.* [Italics added.] He said, 'Look, I've done what I can. . . . You care for him. We're going on!' "

The group quickly clothed the sadhu with extra clothes from their packs and gave him food and water. McCoy continued the trek. His friend, Stephen, stayed with the sadhu.

The Japanese had been lagging behind. When they reached Stephen and discovered the plight of the sadhu, they gave the sadhu food and drink. Stephen then asked their Sherpas to carry the sadhu down to the base camp. *The Sherpas declined. They said that they "would have to exert all their energy to get themselves over the pass. . . . they could not carry a man down 1,000 feet to the hut, reclimb the slope, and get across safely before the snow melted."* [Italics added.]

The Sherpas did manage to carry "the sadhu down to a rock in the sun at about 15,000 feet and pointed out the hut [base camp] another 500 feet below." When Stephen joined up with McCoy, Stephen bitterly reproached him: "How do you feel about contributing to the death of a fellow man?"

Later, when talking about the incident with Stephen, McCoy says, *"What right does an almost naked pilgrim who chooses the wrong trail have to disrupt our lives?"* At the end of his story, McCoy writes, "We do not know if the sadhu lived or died."

ANALYSIS

Lost in the Group

The first trap that seems obvious from the story is the trap *lost in the group*. In his own analysis, McCoy writes, "No one person was willing to assume ultimate responsibility for the sadhu. Each was willing to do his bit just so long as it was not too inconvenient. When it got to be a bother, everyone just passed the buck to someone else and took off."

When we're part of a group, our individual accountability is weakened. With everyone responsible, no one takes ultimate responsibility.

Tyranny of Goals

The next trap that influences this story is *tyranny of goals*. McCoy refers to his trip as "a once-in-a-lifetime opportunity." On another occasion he talks about it as, "one of the most powerful experiences of our lives." Later he says, "If we failed to cross the pass . . . the last half of our . . . trip would be ruined." Undoubtedly, conquering the pass was a highly desirable goal for McCoy. His goal pulled him toward the summit, leaving the sadhu behind. Our goals drive us, because we believe they will make us happy. We forget that feelings of happiness are always transitory. Studies have shown that important accomplishments create euphoria that endures less than three months. Following this short period of good feelings, our level of happiness goes back to what it was prior to the accomplishment.

Time Pressure

Tyranny of goals is reinforced in this story by the trap *time pressure*. To meet their goal and for their own safety, the group needed to cross the pass *"before the sun melted the steps cut in the ice."* The New Zealander who finds the sadhu, the Sherpas who refuse to carry the sadhu to base camp—as well as McCoy—all express this point.

Good ethics take time. When we're pressured by time, we're often not even aware that there might be a potential ethical dilemma. The research that we present in this book that supports *time pressure* is an experiment that creates a challenge very much like the story of the sadhu: seminary students, hurrying to be on time to give an impromptu talk on the Good Samaritan, encounter a victim—collapsed and groaning in an alley. In the *high-hurry condition*, only 10 percent offered help; in the *low-hurry condition*, 63 percent of the seminary students offered help!

Conflicts of Loyalty

When the Sherpas refused to carry the sadhu back to the base camp, they were not only caught in the trap of *time pressure* because of the melting snow but also trapped in *conflicts of loyalty*. They were employed to meet the needs of the trekkers as well as to watch out for their safety. After the porters declined to carry the sadhu, they told Stephen that they "would have to exert all their energy to get themselves over the pass . . . they could not carry a man down 1,000 feet to the hut, reclimb the slope, and get across safely before the snow melted."

McCoy writes, "Our Sherpa . . . was focused on his responsibility for bringing us up the mountain safe and sound."

Self-Serving Bias

At one point in the story, when Stephen and McCoy are talking about the sadhu, McCoy initially takes a defensive stance: "What right does an almost naked pilgrim who chooses the wrong trail have to disrupt our lives?" To lessen his own guilt, McCoy blames the tragedy on the sadhu. He admits that what happened was wrong, but places the culpability on the sadhu's error.

Annihilation of Guilt

Annihilation of guilt is the final trap that causes the abandonment of the sadhu. In the section of this book on *anger*, we related how *anger* could cover up or obliterate our more tender feelings. Our capacity for *empathy* is then reduced, which leads to less guilt. The New Zealander who finds the sadhu is "angry" when he dumps the sadhu's body at the feet of McCoy. His *anger* was probably due to the *time pressure* of the melting snow and perhaps *tyranny of goals*—his desire to conquer the eighteen-thousand-foot Himalayan pass. When an important goal is hindered or blocked, we often get angry.

McCoy writes that one of the reasons he acted unethically was probably due to the "stress"—"a high adrenaline flow" from the danger, "effort," and "altitude." Right after McCoy leaves the sadhu with Stephen to continue his ascent, he writes, "if the ice steps had given way, I would have slid down about 3,000 feet." When we're stressed or feel fear, our system is flooded with adrenaline. Like *anger*, which is also adrenaline-based, an extreme amount of stress or fear can obliterate our more tender feelings, which then reduces our capacity for *empathy* and leads to the *annihilation of guilt*.

JONESTOWN

I N 1 9 7 8, in a South American settlement called Jonestown—named
after its leader Reverend Jim Jones—over nine hundred people committed suicide. Under the leadership of Jones, the communal members
of Jonestown gathered together; for the most part, they administered
a cyanide-laced drink to their children and then drank themselves.
"Their bodies were found lying together, arm in arm."

How could such a horror ever happen? Many of these people were
middle- or upper-middle-class professionals: nurses, lawyers, college
professors, businessmen, social workers.

The story begins about twenty years earlier when Jones established
his church, the Peoples Temple, in Indiana. The Peoples Temple is a
tragedy about how Reverend Jones—little by little—became a cruel
dictator. Over a long period of time, under his directives, members
eventually gave all their personal property and savings to the Peoples
Temple; spouses were forced to sexually degrade their partners, and
parents beat their children to the point of unconsciousness. By the time
his church settled in South America, Jones controlled almost every aspect of the lives of his congregation.

In 1978 a small group of journalists and "concerned relatives" led
by Congressman Leo Ryan visited Jonestown. After a short visit, two
families, members of the Peoples Temple, tried to leave with Ryan
and his group. As they were boarding planes, they were "ambushed

and fired upon by Temple gunman—five people, including Ryan, were murdered."

As the ambush was happening, Jones directed the members of Jonestown to come together. "He informed them that the Congressman's party would be killed and then initiated the final ritual: the 'revolutionary suicide' that the membership had rehearsed on prior occasions."[1]

ANALYSIS

Psychopathy

It's clear that Jim Jones's behavior was psychopathic: (1) frequent deceit, (2) acts of unlawful behavior, (3) aggressiveness, and (4) reckless disregard for safety. To be diagnosed as a psychopath, a person must display this type of behavior since the age of fifteen. It's probable that Jones had these symptoms as a young man. As a child he was severely neglected.

Jim Jones was born in 1931. His father, James Thurman Jones, "was never quite the same" after he returned from serving in the military in the First World War. Some say he had "been exposed to mustard gas. Others say he was just a drunk." Jones's father was committed to a psychiatric hospital for five years in the 1920s.

"When Jimmy was 4 or 5 years old, his mother would give him a sack lunch and send him out of the house. He would wander around town with his lunch, often with a stray dog following him around."[1] "At an early age, he conducted cruel experiments on barnyard animals and tried to control his playmates, locking them up in a barn and later threatening his best friend with a gun."[2]

Obedience to Authority

The story of the Peoples Temple is a history of a congregation obeying the directives of Jones. As one member of the congregation said, "Jim made us do all kinds of weird things. . . . *Jim gave orders and members weren't likely to refuse him.*" [Italics added.][1]

In 1974, for example, when the Peoples Temple was still in California, Jones accused a small woman by the name of Kay Rosas of making a racist comment. Jim asked her to come forward and stand in front of the congregation. When Kay denied the accusation, Jim screamed, "You are a racist. . . . !" He then ordered "twenty" black women sitting in the front "to come forward and form a line." Jones had his bodyguard "put boxing gloves on the first woman."

He then ordered her to give Kay a thrashing. "By the time the fourth woman had taken her turn, Kay fell down, unable to stand. 'Don't let her get off that easy,' Jim shouted. . . . 'Hold her up and make her take it.'. . . . As the women continued to hit Kay her nose began to bleed, and blood was dripping on her clothes, but still the women kept coming. . . ." A member of the cult later wrote, "The look of horror on the faces of the black women . . . those faces were to remain in my memory for years to come. Jim had turned sweet women into monsters, attacking a helpless victim, *just by his command.*" [Italics added.][2]

Stanley Milgram, who conducted the experiment on *obedience to authority* (Trap 1), was indeed right when he concluded that obedience is an "impulse overriding training in ethics, sympathy, and moral conduct."[3]

Justification

Jones frequently used "the Cause" as a *justification* for his actions. Jeanie Mills, a former member of the Peoples Temple, writes in her book *Six Years with God*, "For the thousandth time, I rationalized my doubts. If Jim feels it's necessary for the Cause, who am I to question his wisdom?" On another occasion she writes, "We were learning a new set of ethics from Jim . . . called 'situational ethics'. . . . You do whatever Jim says because he knows what is needed for the Cause. Whenever he suggested something that sounded . . . dishonest, he would lovingly remind the congregation of the Cause and tell us not to worry."[1] What was "the Cause"? In sermons to his congregation, Jones explained his *justification*:

I have seen by divine revelation the total annihilation of this country and many other parts of the world. . . . The only survivors will be those people who are hidden in the cave that I have been shown in a vision. Those who go into this cave with me will be saved from the poisonous radioactive fallout that will follow the nuclear bomb attack. . . . It will be up to our group to begin life anew on this continent. Then we will begin a truly ideal society. . . . I have come for a special mission and you who are following me are my chosen people. . . . I have the answers to the problems of society. . . . I will eliminate racism, political oppression, ecological imbalances, and the problem of the superrich and the superpoor.[2]

In the late 1960s, because of the threat from Russia, nuclear annihilation was a real possibility. Children in elementary schools in the 1950s experienced nuclear attack drills at school: "duck and cover." Many of them, including coauthor Robert Hoyk, remember having nightmares of mushroom clouds; as teens in the 1960s, they often thought they would never reach the age of thirty because of a nuclear holocaust. Because of nuclear threat and the promise of "peace on earth," Jim's "Cause" inspired his congregation. As Tim Stoen, lawyer and former member of the Peoples Temple stated, "I wanted utopia so damn bad I could die."[3]

Desensitization

Our nervous system has the capacity to get used to painful emotions. If we act unethically we feel guilt and shame. If we repeat the same behavior more than once, the guilt and shame begin to deaden—to have less impact. In a section of her book, Jeannie Mills describes how Jones began overtly talking about sexual encounters he had with members of his cult. Mills then writes, "The first time Jim had talked like this, people were shocked, *but like everything else he did, after a few times, it ceased to be shocking.*" [Italics added.][1] With repetition, members of the cult became desensitized to Jones's unethical behavior.

Conformity

The influence of *conformity* was always an undercurrent in the Peoples Temple. As one cult member stated, "Fear, lack of sleep and *continual group pressure* had supplanted reasonable thought." [Italics added.][1]

A tape that was recorded during the final act of suicide reveals the power of *conformity*:

Woman: But I'm afraid to die.
Jones: I don't think you are. I don't think you are.
Woman: I look at all the babies and I think they deserve to live.

Jones: But they deserve much more—they deserve peace. The best testimony
we can give is to leave this . . . world. (*Applause*)

First Man: It's over sister. . . . We've made a beautiful day. (*Applause*)

Second Man: If you tell us we have to give our lives now, we're ready. (*Applause*) [Italics added.][2]

Notice the "applause" of the group—the tyranny and reign of *conformity* was evident and brutal.

Conformity Pressure

As you might remember, if just one person dissents in a group, the pressure to conform is broken. Jones used his authority, intimidation, and punishment to prevent dissent. As Jeannie Mills writes, "There was an unwritten but perfectly understood law in the church that was very important: No one is to criticize Father [Jones], his wife, or his children. . . . Any voice of criticism was called treason. A word against Jim was called blasphemy." Even before the Peoples Temple moved to Jonestown, Jones's staff could not disagree with his opinion nor his directives, "even in private."[1] A survivor of the Peoples Temple, Deborah Blakey, stated: "Although I felt terrible about what was happening, I was afraid to say anything because I knew that anyone with a differing opinion gained the wrath of Jones and other members."[2]

Small Steps

By the time Jones moved his congregation to the settlement in South America, he had ultimate control over his congregation. His control was gained over a period of many years by demanding more and more of his followers in small increments. Research demonstrates that if someone complies with a small request, they're more apt to comply with a larger request in the future. Let's look at the mass suicide as a case in point.

Step One   The first small step that Jones took was asking the members of his congregation to vote: "How many of you here today would be willing to take your own lives now to keep the church from being discredited? We could leave a note saying that we were doing this as a sign that we want peace on earth. . . ." Jones then compiled a list of people who weren't ready to die and read the list to the congregation: "The names I have just read are people who can't be trusted yet. A person is not trustworthy until he is fully ready to lay down his life for this Cause."[1]

Step Two Two years later, Jones began a number of false suicide enactments. He would give members a glass of wine and, after they had finished drinking, declare that the wine had been laced with poison and that they would die quickly. After forty-five minutes or so, he would then tell them it was just a "test." Jones would say to them, "I have tested you all tonight. As you were reacting, I had my staff watching each of your faces to determine if you were indeed ready to die. I know now which of you can be trusted and which of you cannot."[2]

Step Three After the Peoples Temple moved to Jonestown, ritual suicide, called "White Nights," was rehearsed repeatedly. In the middle of the night, sirens would go off. Members would never know until it was over if it was the real thing. "A mass meeting would ensue. . . . we would be told that the jungle was swarming with mercenaries. . . . we were given a small glass of red liquid to drink. We were told that the liquid contained poison and that we would die within 45 minutes."[3]

Doing Is Believing

The more members of the Peoples Temple practiced ritualistic suicide ("White Nights"), the more they began to believe in it. They observed their own behavior, which informed them of their beliefs. Research has demonstrated that if we *act as if* we are happy, angry, sad—we will actually experience these emotions. What we do is what we believe. The more the members of the Peoples Temple *acted as if* they were committing suicide—the more they identified with the role they were playing.

Moments before the actual mass suicide took place, a member of the church—one of Jim's guards—came up to Charles Garry, a hired lawyer for the People's Temple, and exclaimed, "It's a great moment. . . . we all die."[1]

On the body of a woman who had drunk the poison and died, a message written on her arm in her last hours stated, "Jim Jones is the only one."[2]

By chance, one member survived Jonestown because she was away at a dental appointment when the mass suicide was enacted. Later in an interview she stated, "If I had been there, I would have been the first one to stand in that line and take that poison and I would have been proud to take it. The thing I'm sad about is this; that I missed the ending."[3]

Although some members were forced to take the poison, the vast majority of members drank the poison willingly. By having *rehearsed* ritualistic suicide, members believed in "the ending." What we do, we believe.

Renaming

Renaming—euphemistic language that tends to minimize, sanitize, or even exalt transgressions—was also prevalent at Jonestown. A guard tower was referred to as a "playground."[1] Instead of using the word *death*, Jones often talked about "stepping over."[2] As previously stated, suicide drills were called "White Nights," and the act of suicide itself was renamed as "a revolutionary act."[3]

FINAL WORDS

IT'S IRONIC that most of the research described in this book about ethics uses deception. There are so many influences that happen simultaneously to cause unethical behavior that conclusions are pure guesswork. It is only through experimental research, by strictly controlling the circumstances, that we can take each influence one at a time without the others to see if it indeed has an impact. Deception is one way research tightly controls the circumstances.

The difference is, deception in research is scrutinized before each study and revealed afterward. Today, all research done in universities must be reviewed by an ethics committee before the researcher is allowed to proceed. Deception is only used if the committee makes the judgment that the benefit of the potential gain of knowledge outweighs the effect of deception on the subjects. At the end of the experiment, subjects are always debriefed, that is, the purpose of the experiment and the deception used are explained to them in detail. They are left with the truth.

THIS BOOK OFFERS a taxonomy of traps that can be used to analyze ethical dilemmas and issues. The analysis may be done informally in the context of our personal lives or more officially in business meetings or other organizational forums.

The traps in this book often involve self-deception. This taxonomy gives us leverage to perceive the truth by identifying the group and individual illusions we have fallen prey to. It gives us a language to identify present or future dangers. When we clearly identify danger, we can prepare for it and avoid it.

Most of the traps in this book are based on scientific evidence. Having a taxonomy takes the study of ethics out of the realm of philosophy and intentions and puts it into the realm of science and practical awareness. Our hope is that with time, other traps will be identified and the present taxonomy will grow in richness and complexity.

QUESTIONS OR COMMENTS? E-mail author Robert Hoyk at: bobhoyk@earthlink.net.

TRAPPED!

1. John C. Maxwell, *There's No Such Thing as Business Ethics* (New York: Warner Books, 2003), 1.

2. Ibid., 2.

3. Roben Farzad, "Jail Terms for 2 at Top of Adelphia," *The New York Times*, June 21, 2005.

4. Maxwell, *There's No Such Thing as Business Ethics*, 2.

5. Andrew Ross Sorkin, "Ex-Tyco Officers Get 8 to 25 Years," *The New York Times*, September 20, 2005, p. A1.

6. Wallace Immen, "Do You Work for a Psychopath?" *The Globe and Mail*, August 17, 2005, p. C1.

7. Jeffrey L. Seglin, *The Right Thing: Conscience, Profit and Personal Responsibility in Today's Business* (London: Spiro Press, 2003), 9.

8. Jeffrey L. Seglin, *The Good, the Bad, and Your Business: Choosing Right When Ethical Dilemmas Pull You Apart* (New York: John Wiley & Sons, 2000), 54.

9. Jeffrey L. Seglin, "The Right Thing: A Company Credo, as Applied or Not," *The New York Times*, July 15, 2001.

10. KPMG, "2000 Organizational Integrity Survey: A Summary," 2000, p. 2, available at www.uskpmg.com.

11. Ken Belson, "Ex-Chief of WorldCom Is Found Guilty in $11 Billion Fraud: Ebbers Has Become Highest Executive to be Convicted," *The New York Times*, March 16, 2005, p. 1; Ken Belson, "WorldCom Head Is Given 25 Years for Huge Fraud," *The New York Times*, July 14, 2005, p. 1.

WHY DO TRAPS EXIST, AND WHAT ARE THEY?

1. J. Platt, "Social Traps," *American Psychologist* (August 1973): 641.

WHY THIS ISN'T JUST ANOTHER BUSINESS ETHICS BOOK

1. Laura L. Nash, "Ethics Without the Sermon," *Harvard Business Review on Corporate Ethics* (Boston: Harvard Business School Publishing Corporation, 2003), 44–45.

2. Linda Klebe Trevino, "Moral Reasoning and Business Ethics: Implications for Research, Education, and Management," *Journal of Business Ethics* 11 (1992): 445–459.

3. J. L. Badaracco and A. P. Webb, "Business Ethics: A View from the Trenches," *California Management Review* 37, no. 2 (1995): 8–28.

4. Ibid.

5. Badaracco and Webb, "Business Ethics."

6. Ibid.

TRAP 1: OBEDIENCE TO AUTHORITY

1. Stanley Milgram, "Behavioral Study of Obedience," *The Journal of Abnormal and Social Psychology*, 67, no. 4 (1963): 371–378, American Psychological Association, copyright renewed 1991 by Alexandra Milgram; Andrew Michener, John DeLamater, Shalom Schwartz, and Robert Merton, *Social Psychology: Second Edition* (New York: Harcourt Brace Jovanovich, 1990), 389–391.

2. Associated Press, "Former WorldCom Executive Says Ebber Offered Apology," *The New York Times*, January 28, 2005, p. C5.

TRAP 2: SMALL STEPS

1. Peter Fusaro and Ross Miller, *What Went Wrong at Enron* (Hoboken, NJ: John Wiley & Sons, 2002), 129–132, reprinted with permission of John Wiley & Sons, Inc.; Kurt Eichenwald, *Conspiracy of Fools* (New York: Broadway Books, 2005), 163.

2. David Myers, *Social Psychology*, 7th Edition, McGraw-Hill Higher Education, 2002. Reproduced with permission of The McGraw-Hill Companies.

SIDESTEPPING RESPONSIBILITY

1. S. H. Schwartz, *Moral Orientations and Interpersonal Conduct in Moral Encounters*, doctoral dissertation, University of Michigan (Ann Arbor: University Microfilms, 1967), No. 67-15,690. Cited in Shalom Schwartz, "Words, Deeds, and the Perception of Consequences and Responsibility in Action Situations," *Journal of Personality and Social Psychology* 10, no. 3 (1968): 232–242; Daniel Batson and others, "In a Very Different Voice: Unmasking Moral Hypocrisy," *Journal of Personality and Social Psychology*, 72, no. 6 (1997): 1335–1348.

Trap 3: Indirect Responsibility

1. David Myers, *Social Psychology*, 7th Edition, McGraw-Hill Higher Education, 2002. Reproduced with permission of The McGraw-Hill Companies.

2. Ibid.

Trap 4: Faceless Victims

1. David Myers, *Social Psychology*, 7th Edition, McGraw-Hill Higher Education, 2002.

2. Douglas Birsch and John Fielder, *The Ford Pinto Case: A Study in Applied Ethics, Business, and Technology* (Albany, NY: State University of New York Press, 1994), 16, 51, 52, 58, 104.

3. Ibid.

4. F. T. Cullen, W. J. Maakestad, and G. Cavender, *Corporate Crime Under Attack* (Chicago: Anderson Publishing, 1987), 164.

Trap 5: Lost in the Group

1. David Myers, *Social Psychology*, 7th Edition, McGraw-Hill Higher Education, 2002.

2. Albert Bandura and others, "Disinhibition of Aggression Through Diffusion of Responsibility and Dehumanization of Victims," *Journal of Research in Personality* 9 (1975): 253–269.

TRAP 6: COMPETITION

1. James Surowiecki, "The Financial Page: Team Players," *The New Yorker*, May 10, 2004, p. 41.

2. Robert Wright, *Nonzero: The Logic of Human Destiny* (New York: Vintage Books, 2000), 5–6.

3. Andrew Michener, John DeLamater, Shalom Schwartz, and Robert Merton, *Social Psychology*, 2nd ed. (New York: Harcourt Brace Jovanovich, 1990), 72.

4. L. Kohlberg, L. (1969). "Stage and Sequence: The Cognitive-Developmental Approach to Socialization," in *Handbook of Socialization Theory and Research*, ed. D. Goslin (Chicago: Rand McNally, 1969).

5. Peter Fusaro and Ross Miller, *What Went Wrong at Enron* (Hoboken, NJ: John Wiley & Sons, 2002), 51–52. Reprinted with Permission of John Wiley & Sons, Inc.

6. Robert Blake and Jane Mouton, "Reactions to Intergroup Competition Under Win-Lose Conditions," *Management Science* 7, no. 1 (1960): 420–435; Robert Blake and Jane Mouton, "Intergroup Problem Solving in Organizations: From Theory to Practice," in *The Social Psychology of Intergroup Relations*, ed. William Austin and Stephen Worchel (Pacific Grove, CA: Brooks/Cole, 1979), 19–32.

SELF-INTEREST

1. Doug Lennick and Fred Kiel, *Moral Intelligence: Enhancing Business Performance and Leadership Success* (Upper Saddle River, NJ: Pearson Education, 2005), 32.

2. *Morning Monitor* (Springfield, IL, 1880–1892). Cited in Daniel Batson and others, "Where Is the Altruism in the Altruistic Personality?" *Journal of Personality and Social Psychology* 50 no. 1 (1986): 212.

Trap 7: Tyranny of Goals

1. Gwynn Nettler, *Lying, Cheating, Stealing* (Cincinnati: Anderson Publishing, 1982), 21–22.

2. Ibid., 84.

3. Robert Wright, "Dancing to Evolution's Tune," *Time*, January 17, 2005, p. A11.

4. Ibid.

5. Martin Seligman, *Authentic Happiness* (New York: Free Press, 2002), 48.

6. Philip Brickman and others, "Lottery Winners and Accident Victims: Is Happiness Relative?" *Journal of Personality and Social Psychology* 36 (1978): 917–927.

Trap 8: Money

1. Jim Warner, *Aspirations of Greatness: Mapping the Midlife Leader's Reconnection to Self and Soul* (New York: John Wiley & Sons, 2002), 303, 305.

2. Ed Diener and others, "The Relationship Between Income and Subjective Well-Being: Relative or Absolute?" *Social Indicators Research* 28 (1993): 195–223.

3. R. A. Easterlin, "Explaining Happiness," *Proceedings of the National Academy of Sciences*, September 16, 2003, Vol. 100, No. 19, 1176–1183.

4. Warner, *Aspirations of Greatness*, 9.

5. Peter Fusaro and Ross Miller, *What Went Wrong at Enron* (Hoboken, NJ: John Wiley & Sons, 2002), 40, 49–50.

Trap 9: Conflicts of Interest

1. Ken Belson, "Ex-Chief of WorldCom Is Found Guilty in $11 Billion Fraud: Ebbers Has Become Highest Executive to Be Convicted," *The New York Times*, March 16, 2005, p. 1; Ken Belson, "WorldCom's Audacious Failure and Its Toll on an Industry," *The New York Times*, January 18, 2005, p. C1.

2. Ken Belson, "WorldCom Complexity an Issue at Trial," *The New York Times*, January 27, 2005, p. C4; Belson, "WorldCom's Audacious Failure," p. C1.

3. Gretchen Morgenson, "Pennies That Aren't from Heaven," *The New York Times*, November 7, 2004. Copyright © 2004 by The New York Times Company. Reprinted with permission.

4. Associated Press, "Ex-WorldCom Accountant Says She Was Told to Falsify Entries," *The New York Times*, February 3, 2005, p. C14.

5. John Cassidy, "The Investigation: How Eliot Spitzer Humbled Wall Street," *The New Yorker*, April 7, 2003, pp. 55–73.

6. Marcia Vickers and others, "How Corrupt Is Wall Street?" *BusinessWeek*, May 13, 2002, pp. 37–42, 132.

7. Joseph B. Treaster, "How Old Ties Helped Wrap Up the Marsh Deal," *The New York Times*, February 5, 2005, p. B1.

8. Joseph Treaster, "Aon Will Pay $190 Million To Settle Complaints on Bids," *The New York Times*, March 5, 2005, p. B3.

TRAP 10: CONFLICTS OF LOYALTY

1. Laura L. Nash, "Ethics Without the Sermon," *Harvard Business Review on Corporate Ethics* (Boston: Harvard Business School Publishing Corporation, 2003), 31.

2. Joseph Badaracco Jr., *Business Ethics: Roles and Responsibilities* (Boston: Harvard Business School Publishing Corporation, 1995), 22–25.

TRAP 11

1. Solomon Asch, "Opinions and Social Pressure," *Scientific American* 193, no. 5 (1955): 31–35; Andrew Michener, John DeLamater, Shalom Schwartz, and Robert Merton, *Social Psychology*, 2nd ed. (New York: Harcourt Brace Jovanovich, 1990), 354–356.

TRAP 12: CONFORMITY PRESSURE

1. Lynn Sharp Paine, "Managing for Organizational Integrity," in *Harvard Business Review on Corporate Ethics* (Boston: Harvard Business School Publishing Corporation, 2003), 90.

TRAP 13: "DON'T MAKE WAVES"

1. William Whyte Jr., *The Organization Man* (New York: Simon and Schuster, 1956), 120–122.

2. Jay Lorsch and Elizabeth MacIver, *Pawns or Potentates: The Reality of America's Corporate Boards* (Boston: Harvard Business School Press, 1989). Cited in Joseph Badaracco Jr., *Business Ethics: Roles and Responsibilities* (Boston: Harvard Business School Publishing Corporation, 1995), 279.

3. Kurt Eichenwald, "In String of Corporate Troubles, Critics Focus on Boards' Failings," *The New York Times*, September 21, 2003, p. 1.

4. James Surowiecki, "The Financial Page: Board Stiffs," *The New Yorker*, March 8, 2004, p. 30.

5. Lynne Jeter, *Disconnected: Deceit and Betrayal at WorldCom* (Hoboken, NJ: John Wiley & Sons, 2003), 198–199. Reprinted with permission of John Wiley & Sons, Inc.

TRAP 14: SELF-ENHANCEMENT

1. C. Crossen, "American Opinion: Rate Your Own Morals and Values on a Scale from One to 100 (100 Being Perfect)," *Wall Street Journal* (eastern edition), December 13, 1996, p. R4.

2. Personal communication, Constance Dalenberg, December 2, 2005.

TRAP 15: TIME PRESSURE

1. Anthony Parinello, *Think and Sell Like a CEO* (n.a.: Entrepreneur Media, 2002), 53.

2. From *Selling to VITO*, Copyright © 1994, 1999, Parinello, Inc. Used by permission of Adams Media, an F+W Publications, Inc. All rights reserved.

3. Lynne Jeter, *Disconnected: Deceit and Betrayal at WorldCom* (Hoboken, NJ: John Wiley & Sons, 2003), p. 129. Reprinted with permission of John Wiley & Sons, Inc.

4. John Darley and Daniel Batson, "From Jerusalem to Jericho: A Study of Situational and Dispositional Variables in Helping Behavior," *The Journal of Personality and Social Psychology* 27 no. 1 (1973): 100–108. Copyright © 1973 by the American Psychological Association. Reproduced with permission.

TRAP 16: DECISION SCHEMAS

1. Dennis Gioia, cited in Douglas Birsch and John Fielder, *The Ford Pinto Case: A Study in Applied Ethics, Business, and Technology* (Albany, NY: State University of New York Press, 1994), pp. 51, 52, 58, 97–114.

2. Ibid.

3. Ibid.

4. Douglas Birsch and John Fielder, *The Ford Pinto Case: A Study in Applied Ethics, Business, and Technology* (Albany, NY: State University of New York Press, 1994), 58, 97–114.

TRAP 17: ENACTING A ROLE

1. David Myers, *Social Psychology*, 7th Edition, McGraw-Hill Higher Education, 2002. Reproduced with permission of The McGraw-Hill Companies.

2. P. G. Zimbardo, "The Stanford Prison Experiment," 1972. A slide and tape presentation produced by Philip G. Zimbardo, Inc., P.O. Box 4395, Stanford, California, 94305.

3. Myers, *Social Psychology*.

4. Laura L. Nash, "Ethics Without the Sermon," *Harvard Business Review on Corporate Ethics* (Boston: Harvard Business School Publishing Corporation, 2003), 44–45.

5. Peter Fusaro and Ross Miller, *What Went Wrong at Enron* (Hoboken, NJ: John Wiley & Sons, 2002), p. 28. Reprinted with permission of John Wiley & Sons, Inc.

6. From *The Smartest Guys in the Room* by Bethany McLean and Peter Elkind, copyright © 2003 by *Fortune*, a division of Time, Inc. Used by permission of Portfolio, an imprint of Penguin Group (USA), Inc.

TRAP 18: POWER

1. David Kipnis, *The Powerholders* (Chicago: University of Chicago Press, 1976), 168–212.

2. Lynn Sharp Paine, "Managing for Organizational Integrity," *Harvard Business Review on Corporate Ethics* (Boston: Harvard Business School Publishing Corporation, 2003), 44–45.

3. Paine, "Managing for Organizational Integrity."

TRAP 19: JUSTIFICATION

1. Ervin Staub, "The Origins and Prevention of Genocide, Mass Killing, and Other Collective Violence," *Peace and Conflict: Journal of Peace Psychology* 5, no. 4 (1999): 303–336.

2. Robert L. Heilbroner, *In the Name of Profit: Profiles in Corporate Irresponsibility* (New York: Doubleday, 1972). Cited in Kermit Vandivier, "The Aircraft Brake Scandal," *Harper's Magazine* 244 (1972): 45–52.

3. Ibid.

4. Timothy Brock and Arnold Buss, "Effects of Justification for Aggression and Communication with the Victim on Postaggression Dissonance," *Journal of Abnormal and Social Psychology* 68, no. 4 (1964): 403–412.

5. Ibid.

TRAP 20: OBLIGATION

1. Timothy Brock and Arnold Buss, "Effects of Justification for Aggression and Communication with the Victim on Postaggression Dissonance," *Journal of Abnormal and Social Psychology* 68, no. 4 (1964): 403–412.

Trap 21: Anger

1. Daniel Goldman, *Emotional Intelligence* (New York: Bantam Books, 1995), 105–110.

2. Martin Hoffman, "Empathy, Role Taking, Guilt, and Development of Altruistic Motives," in *Moral Development and Behavior: Theory, Research, and Social Issues*, ed. Thomas Lickona (New York: Holt, Rinehart and Winston, 1976), 126.

3. Ibid., 139.

4. Paul Miller and Nancy Eisenberg, "The Relation of Empathy to Aggressive and Externalizing/Antisocial Behavior," *Psychological Bulletin* 103, no. 3 (1988): 324–344.

5. Kurt Eichenwald, "No Certainties in Enron Plea," *The New York Times*, December 29, 2005, p. 1. Copyright © 2005 by The New York Times Company. Reprinted with permission.

Trap 23: Alcohol

1. Joel Cooper and Robert Croyle, "Attitudes and Attitude Change," *Annual Review of Psychology* 35 (1984): 395–426.

2. Lynne Jeter, *Disconnected: Deceit and Betrayal at WorldCom* (Hoboken, NJ: John Wiley & Sons, 2003), 91. Reprinted with permission of John Wiley & Sons, Inc.

Trap 24: Desensitization

1. From *The Smartest Guys in the Room* by Bethany McLean and Peter Elkind, copyright © 2003 by *Fortune*, a division of Time, Inc. Used by permission of Portfolio, an imprint of Penguin Group (USA), Inc.

Trap 25: Reduction Words

1. Jeffrey Toobin, "The Bench: An Agreeable Witness," *The New Yorker*, June 30, 2003, pp.39–40; Jeffrey Toobin, "The Bench: Star Witness," *The New Yorker*, February 16 and 23, 2004, pp. 66, 68.

2. Constance Hays, "5 Months in Jail, and Stewart Vows, 'I'll Be Back,'" *The New York Times*, July 17, 2004, p. 1.

3. William E. Adams, *The Choices Program: How to Stop Hurting the People Who Love You* (Long Beach, CA: Author, 2003), 27.

Trap 26: Renaming

1. Albert Bandura and others, "Mechanisms of Moral Disengagement in the Exercise of Moral Agency," *Journal of Personality and Social Psychology* 71, no. 2 (1996): 364–374.

2. Richard Oppel Jr., "Enron Traders on Grandma Millie and Making Out Like Bandits," *The New York Times*, June 13, 2004, The World, p. 14. Copyright © 2004 by The New York Times Company. Reprinted with permission.

Traps 27 and 28: Advantageous Comparison and Zooming Out

1. Albert Bandura and others, "Mechanisms of Moral Disengagement in the Exercise of Moral Agency," *Journal of Personality and Social Psychology* 71, no. 2 (1996): 364–374.

2. Michael Lewis, *Liar's Poker* (New York: Penguin Books, 1990).

Trap 29: "Everybody Does It"

1. Thomas Gabor, *Everybody Does It* (Toronto: University of Toronto Press, 1994), 183.

2. Gina Agostinelli and others, "Self-Protection and Self-Enhancement Biases in Estimates of Population Prevalence," *Personality and Social Psychology Bulletin* 18, no. 5 (1992): 631–642.

Trap 30: "We Won't Get Caught"

1. Joseph Badaracco Jr., *Business Ethics: Roles and Responsibilities* (Boston: Harvard Business School, 1995), 62–65.

Trap 31: "We Didn't Hurt Them That Bad"

1. Timothy Brock and Arnold Buss, "Effects of Justification for Aggression and Communication with the Victim on Postaggression Dissonance," *Journal of Abnormal and Social Psychology* 68, no. 4 (1964): 403–412.

Trap 32: Self-Serving Bias

1. Keith Campbell and Constantine Sedikides, "Self-Threat Magnifies the Self-Serving Bias: A Meta-Analytic Integration," *Review of General Psychology* 3, no. 1 (1999): 23–43.

2. Albert Bandura and others, "Mechanisms of Moral Disengagement in the Exercise of Moral Agency," *Journal of Personality and Social Psychology* 71, no. 2 (1996): 364–374.

3. Ibid.

4. Jeffrey L. Seglin, "The Right Thing: A Blame Game Hurts Both Ford and Firestone," *The New York Times*, June 17, 2001. Copyright © 2001 by The New York Times Company. Reprinted with permission.

TRAP 33: ADDICTION

1. *The Gentlemen Conspirators: The Story of Price-Fixers in the Electrical Industry* by John Fuller. Copyright © 1962 by Grove Press, Inc., 1990 by John Grant Fuller. Used by Permission of Grove/Atlantic, Inc.

TRAP 34: COWORKER REACTIONS

1. Ervin Staub, "The Origins and Prevention of Genocide, Mass Killing, and Other Collective Violence," *Peace and Conflict: Journal of Peace Psychology* 5, no. 4 (1999): 303–336.

2. Thomas Gabor, *Everybody Does It* (Toronto: University of Toronto Press, 1994) 197–198.

3. Joseph Badaracco Jr., "We Don't Need Another Hero," *Harvard Business Review on Corporate Ethics* (Boston: Harvard Business School Publishing Corporation, 2003), p.15.

TRAP 35: ESTABLISHED IMPRESSIONS

1. Lee Ross and others, "Perseverance in Self-Perception and Social Perception: Biased Attributional Processes in the Debriefing Paradigm," *Journal of Personality and Social Psychology* 32, no. 5 (1975): 880–892.

2. Robert Hare, *Without Conscience: The Disturbing World of the Psychopaths Among Us* (New York: Guilford Press, 1993), 116–118.

TRAP 36: CONTEMPT FOR THE VICTIM

1. Albert Bandura, "Social Cognitive Theory of Moral Thought and Action," in *Handbook of Moral Behavior and Development Volume 1: Theory*, ed. W. Kurtines and J. Gewirtz (Hillsdale, NJ: Lawrence Erlbaum, 1991), 88.

2. Albert Bandura and others, "Disinhibition of Aggression Through Diffusion of Responsibility and Dehumanization of Victims," *Journal of Research in Personality* 9 (1975): 253–269.

3. Michael Lewis, *Liar's Poker* (New York: Penguin Books, 1990).

4. Robert Wright, *The Moral Animal* (New York: Vintage Books, 1994), 273.

5. S. Milgram, *Obdience to Authority* (New York: Harper and Row, 1974), 10.

TRAP 37: DOING IS BELIEVING

1. David Myers, *Social Psychology*, 7th Edition, McGraw-Hill Higher Education, 2002. Reproduced with permission of The McGraw-Hill Companies.

2. Eric Storch and Jason Storch, "Academic Dishonesty and Attitudes Towards Academic Dishonest Acts: Support for Cognitive Dissonance Theory," *Psychological Reports* 92 (2003): 174–176.

3. From *The Smartest Guys in the Room* by Bethany McLean and Peter Elkind, copyright © 2003 by *Fortune*, a division of Time, Inc. Used by Permission of Portfolio, an imprint of Penguin Group (USA) Inc.

TRAP 38: PSYCHOPATHY

1. Robert Hare, *Without Conscience: The Disturbing World of the Psychopaths Among Us* (New York: Guilford Press, 1993), 3–5.

2. Ibid., 74.

3. *Diagnostic and Statistical Manual of Mental Disorders*, 4th ed. (Washington, DC: American Psychiatric Association, 1994), 649–650.

4. Harold Kaplan and others, *Kaplan and Sadock's Synopsis of Psychiatry Behavioral Sciences Clinical Psychiatry*, 7th ed. (Baltimore: Williams & Wilkins, 1994), 737, 798–799.

5. Martin Seligman, *What You Can Change and What You Can't: The Complete Guide to Successful Self-Improvement* (New York: Fawcett Columbine, 1995, 41–43; David Lykken, *Happiness: What Studies on Twins Show Us About Nature, Nurture, and the Happiness Set-Point* (New York: Golden Books, 1999, 37–38.

6. Seligman, *What You Can Change*, 44.

7. Ibid.

8. "Professional Notes," *Psychotherapy Finances*, December 2004, Juno Beach, FL: Ridgewood Financial Institute, p. 12.

9. Harold Kaplan and others, *Kaplan and Sadock's Synopsis*, 799.

TRAPS 39 AND 40: POVERTY AND NEGLECT

1. Arnold Rogow and Harold Lasswell, *Power, Corruption, and Rectitude* (Englewood Cliffs, NJ: Prentice-Hall, 1963), 44–54.

TRAP 41: LOW SELF-ESTEEM

1. David Myers, *Social Psychology*, 7th Edition, McGraw-Hill Higher Education, 2002. Reproduced with permission of The McGraw-Hill Companies.

2. Bella DePaulo and others, "Lying in Everyday Life," *Journal of Personality and Social Psychology* 70, no. 5 (1996): 979–995; Deborah Kashy and Bella DePaulo, "Who Lies?" *Journal of Personality and Social Psychology* 70, no. 5 (1996): 1037–1051.

3. Elliot Aronson and David Mettee, "Dishonest Behavior as a Function of Differential Levels of Induced Self-Esteem," *Journal of Personality and Social Psychology* 9, no. 2 (1968): 121–127.

TRAP 42: AUTHORITARIANISM

1. David Myers, *Social Psychology*, 7th Edition, McGraw-Hill Higher Education, 2002. Reproduced with permission of The McGraw-Hill Companies.

2. Bob Altemeyer, *The Authoritarian Specter* (Cambridge: Harvard University Press, 1996).

TRAP 43: SOCIAL DOMINANCE ORIENTATION

1. Felicia Pratto, Jim Sidanius, Lisa M. Stallworth, and Bertram F. Malle, "Social Dominance Orientation: A Personality Variable Predicting Social and Political Attitudes," *Journal of Personality and Social Psychology* 67, no. 4 (1994): 741–763.

2. Ibid.

TRAP 44: NEED FOR CLOSURE

1. A. W. Kruglanski, *Lay Epistemics and Human Knowledge: Cognitive and Motivational Bases* (New York: Plenum Press, 1989), 14. Reprinted with kind permission of Springer Science and Business Media.

2. Arie Kruglanski and others, "Motivated Resistance and Openness to Persuasion in the Presence or Absence of Prior Information," *Journal of Personality and Social Psychology* 65, no. 5 (1993): 861–876.

3. Arie Kruglanski and Donna Webster, "Motivated Closing of the Mind: Seizing and Freezing," *Psychological Review* 103, no. 2 (1996): 263–283.

TRAP 45: EMPATHY

1. Lea Winerman, "Mirror Neurons: Building Human Culture Through Mimicry and Empathy," in *Monitor on Psychology* (Washington, DC: American Psychological Association, 2005), 49.

2. M. H. Davis, "Measuring Individual Differences in Empathy: Evidence for a Multidimensional Approach," *Journal of Personality and Social Psychology* 44 (1983): 113–126. Copyright 1980, Mark H. Davis.

3. Daniel Batson and others, "Immorality from Empathy-Induced Altruism: When Compassion and Justice Conflict," *Journal of Personality and Social Psychology* 68, no. 6 (1995): 1042–1054.

"THE PARABLE OF THE SADHU"

1. Bowen McCoy, "The Parable of the Sadhu," *Harvard Business Review on Corporate Ethics* (Boston: Harvard Business School Publishing Corporation, 2003), 165–181.

JONESTOWN

1. Neal Osherow, "Making Sense of the Nonsensical: An Analysis of Jonestown," in *Readings About the Social Animal*, ed. Elliot Aronson (New York: W.H. Freeman, 1992), 68–86; Jeannie Mills, *Six Years with God: Life Inside Reverend Jim Jones's Peoples Temple* (New York: A&W Publishers, 1979).

Psychopathy

1. Don Lattin, "Jonestown: 25 Years Later: How Spiritual Journey Ended in Destruction," *San Francisco Chronicle*, November 18, 2003.

2. Tim Reiterman, "Hell's 25-Year Echo: The Jonestown Mass Suicide," *Los Angeles Times*, November 19, 2003, p. B1.

Obedience to Authority

1. Jeannie Mills, *Six Years with God: Life Inside Reverend Jim Jones's Peoples Temple* (New York: A&W Publishers, 1979), p. 26.

2. Ibid., 279.

3. Stanley Milgram, "Behavioral Study of Obedience," in *Readings About the Social Animal*, ed. Elliot Aronson (New York: W.H. Freeman, 1992), 23–36.

Justification

1. Jeannie Mills, *Six Years with God: Life Inside Reverend Jim Jones's Peoples Temple* (New York: A&W Publishers), 1979.

2. Ibid.

3. C. Winfrey, "Why 900 Died in Guyana." *New York Times Magazine*, February 25, 1979.

Desensitization

1. Jeannie Mills, *Six Years with God: Life Inside Reverend Jim Jones's Peoples Temple* (New York: A&W Publishers, 1979), 257.

Conformity

1. Jeannie Mills, *Six Years with God: Life Inside Reverend Jim Jones's Peoples Temple* (New York: A&W Publishers), 1979.

2. "Tape Hints Early Decision by Jones on Mass Suicide," *Baltimore Sun*, March 15, 1979. Cited in Neal Osherow, "Making Sense of the Nonsensical: An Analysis of Jonestown," in *Readings About the Social Animal*, ed. Elliot Aronson (New York: W.H. Freeman, 1992), 68–86.

Conformity Pressure

1. Jeannie Mills, *Six Years with God: Life Inside Reverend Jim Jones's Peoples Temple* (New York: A&W Publishers), 1979.

2. D. Blakey, Affidavit, San Francisco, June 15, 1978. Cited in Neal Osherow, "Making Sense of the Nonsensical: An Analysis of Jonestown," in *Readings About the Social Animal*, ed. Elliot Aronson (New York: W.H. Freeman, 1992), 68–86.

Small Steps

1. Jeannie Mills, *Six Years with God: Life Inside Reverend Jim Jones's Peoples Temple* (New York: A&W Publishers), 1979.

2. Jeannie Mills, *Six Years with God: Life Inside Reverend Jim Jones's Peoples Temple* (New York: A&W Publishers, 1979).

3. Excerpt from pp. 116–117 from *Cults, Faith, Healing and Coercion* by Galanter, M. (1989). By permission of Oxford University Press, Inc.

Doing Is Believing

1. R. J. Lifton, "Appeal of the Death Trip," *New York Times Magazine*, January 7, 1979. Cited in Neal Osherow, "Making Sense of the Nonsensical: An Analysis of Jonestown," in *Readings About the Social Animal*, ed. Elliot Aronson (New York: W.H. Freeman, 1992), 68–86.

2. T. Cahill, "In the Valley of the Shadow of Death," *Rolling Stone*, January 25, 1979. Cited in Osherow, "Making Sense of the Nonsensical," 68–86.

3. N. Gallagher, "Jonestown: The Survivors' Story," *New York Times Magazine*, November 18, 1979. Cited in Osherow, "Making Sense of the Nonsensical," 68–86.

Renaming

1. T. Cahill, "In the Valley of the Shadow of Death," *Rolling Stone*, January 25, 1979. Cited in Neal Osherow, "Making Sense of the Nonsensical: An Analysis of Jonestown," in *Readings About the Social Animal*, ed. Elliot Aronson (New York: W.H. Freeman, 1992), 68–86.

2. Osherow, "Making Sense of the Nonsensical," 68–86.

3. "Tape Hints Early Decision by Jones on Mass Suicide," *Baltimore Sun*, March 15, 1979. Cited in Osherow, "Making Sense of the Nonsensical," 68–86.